LLEWELLYN'S
Little Book of
CRYSTALS

Margaret Ann Lembo is the author of *Chakra Awakening*; *The Essential Guide to Crystals, Minerals and Stones*; *The Angels & Gemstone Guardians Cards*; *Color Your Life with Crystals*; and *Animal Totems and the Gemstone Kingdom*. She is also the creator of a line of award-winning Aroma-Energetic Sprays. She is a spiritual entrepreneur, aromatherapist, and the owner of The Crystal Garden—a bookstore, gift store, and spiritual center in southeast Florida since 1988. Visit her online at www.MargaretAnnLembo.com or www.TheCrystalGarden.com.

This book is dedicated to all the customers of my store, The Crystal Garden, who have taught me through experience over the past four decades. I am grateful.

LLEWELLYN'S
Little Book of
CRYSTALS

MARGARET ANN LEMBO

LLEWELLYN
WOODBURY, MINNESOTA

Llewellyn's Little Book of Crystals © 2025 by Margaret Ann Lembo. All rights reserved. No part of this book may be used or reproduced in any manner whatsoever, including Internet usage, without written permission from Llewellyn Publications, except in the case of brief quotations embodied in critical articles and reviews. No part of this book may be used or reproduced in any manner for the purpose of training artificial intelligence technologies or systems.

FIRST EDITION
First Printing, 2025

Cover cartouche by Freepik
Cover design by Shira Atakpu
Crystal images by Andy Frame
Interior illustration on page 46 by Llewellyn Art Department

Llewellyn Publications is a registered trademark of Llewellyn Worldwide Ltd.

Library of Congress Cataloging-in-Publication Data is pending.

ISBN: 978-0-7387-8015-3

Llewellyn Worldwide Ltd. does not participate in, endorse, or have any authority or responsibility concerning private business transactions between our authors and the public.

All mail addressed to the author is forwarded, but the publisher cannot, unless specifically instructed by the author, give out an address or phone number.

Any Internet references contained in this work are current at publication time, but the publisher cannot guarantee that a specific location will continue to be maintained. Please refer to the publisher's website for links to authors' websites and other sources.

NOTE: The information in this book is not meant to diagnose, treat, prescribe, or substitute consultation with a licensed healthcare professional.

Llewellyn Publications
A Division of Llewellyn Worldwide Ltd.
2143 Wooddale Drive
Woodbury, MN 55125-2989
www.llewellyn.com

Printed in China

GPSR Representation:
UPI-2M PLUS d.o.o., Medulićeva 20, 10000 Zagreb, Croatia,
matt.parsons@upi2mbooks.hr

Contents

Disclaimer vi

Introduction: My Life with Crystals 1

1: Bringing Crystals into Your Life: How to Find Them, How to Care for Them, and More 7

2: Crystals All Day Long 27

3: Forty Crystals and Their Correspondences 43

Conclusion 205

Recommended Reading 207

DISCLAIMER

While best efforts have been used in preparing this book, neither the author nor the publisher shall be held liable or responsible to any person or entity with respect to any loss or damages alleged to have been caused, directly or indirectly, by the information contained herein. Every situation is different, and the advice and strategies contained in this book may not be suitable for you.

In the following pages, you will find recommendations for the use of certain essential oils and herbal remedies. Each body reacts differently to herbs, essential oils, and other items, so results may vary person to person. If you are allergic to any of these oils or herbs, please refrain from use.

Essential oils are potent; use care when handling them. Never ingest essential oils. There are numerous methods of application for essential oils. Avoid prolonged or excessive inhalation. Always dilute essential oils before placing them on your skin. Do not apply the same essential oil for prolonged periods of time. Keep essential oils away from children and pets, as they can be toxic. Consult a medical professional before using essential oils if you are pregnant.

Crystals have varying toxicity levels. Never ingest a crystal. Do not drink water that has had gemstones soaking in it, as unknown and potentially poisonous minerals can leech out of the stone into the water.

INTRODUCTION
My Life with Crystals

Are you ready to use crystals, minerals, and stones to improve your life? You can transform your life if you choose. You can be healthier, happier, and more content—all you need is a crystal. This book will offer exercises, tips, and practices to incorporate the use of crystals in your daily life.

Having crystals around me all the time has benefited my life tremendously. The energies and vibrations of crystals are uplifting. I own and operate a crystal shop, and I love the amazement on the faces of customers when they walk into the main crystal showroom. They tell me they feel like a kid in a candy shop. Working and playing with crystals is a stunning experience, literally—gemstones sparkle and shine and draw you into their matrix. It's a beautiful experience to connect with a specific crystal or, more likely, a spectacular collection of crystals, minerals, and stones.

In this book, you will uncover various methods to use crystals for personal fulfillment and spiritual awareness. There are many ways to use gemstones for self-confidence, courage, better sleep, focus, creativity, and more! That is what this little book is about. But first, I think it would be useful to share some of my experiences with crystals and how I got to where I am today.

I was raised Catholic in Brooklyn and Breezy Point, New York. Like most children, rocks fascinated me when I was young, and I collected them in little boxes over the years alongside my collection of seashells. My training in metaphysics started at a young age. My mother, a devout Catholic, taught me about communication with the plant kingdom and mental telepathy. Yes! We talked to the plants then, and I still talk to the plants (and the insects, birds, and animals) in my garden today. My mom was a prophetic dreamer, so discussing dreams and their meanings was normal in my household. We even read the zodiac column in the *Daily News* every morning.

In addition, my dad's best friend, Vic, introduced me to the power of positive thought and the magic of believing when I was about eight years old. Vic introduced me to Edgar Cayce's teachings. Things have come full circle now because Edgar Cayce's Association of Research and Enlightenment carries my books, decks, and aromatherapy spray blends in its gift shop.

I didn't start out working in the metaphysical world, though. First, I embarked on a financial career. Then, the stock market crashed. This catapulted me out of mortgage banking and into a career in metaphysics, spirituality, crystals, and aromatherapy. This new career chose me—I didn't choose it. In the 1980s, I was invited to participate and invest in a crystal-buying venture with two friends who were off to Arkansas. I invested as a silent partner, but before I knew it, I wasn't so silent. Investing in this venture reignited my childhood interest in collecting and inspired me to learn about the qualities and uses of crystals. This business venture became a huge part of my life. I opened The Crystal Garden in South Florida in August 1988, and using crystals for healing and personal development became my passion.

Once you start your own collection of crystals, you'll get to know them on a personal level; they will feel like good friends who support you. The more I interacted with gemstones by buying and selling them for my store, the more I learned about them. And of course, I learned so much from the customers who

Crystals for Careers in Art

The culinary arts provide people with nourishment via delicious foods. **Apatite** is a perfect companion for chefs. Creating meals transcends just the preparation; focusing on gratitude as you prepare meals allows for more profound assimilation. Apatite also helps you align with and maintain mindfulness, removing thoughts that create chaos. Finally, apatite supports food absorption. **Blue topaz** is the stone of inspiration and harmony, a good match for musicians. Use blue topaz to connect with your muse. It encourages mental clarity and helps you tap into inspiration from higher levels of awareness. **Carnelian** supports the visual artist, including painters, sculptors, and photographers. Whether your art is for decorative, commercial, or fine purposes, carnelian encourages the manifestation of your artistic vision.

frequented The Crystal Garden. Decades of interacting with people about their choice of crystal was the best training ever! Of course, I read books about crystals, but mostly, I observed my customers. When customers would ask me for a stone for a specific purpose, I would direct them to the gemstone displays to pick what they were naturally attracted to. My staff and I still do this all these years later, and it has proven time and again that people are naturally drawn to the stone they need. My customers shared their challenges and issues, and I would observe which stones they chose to help them heal, realign, attract relationships, or create prosperity in their lives.

Synchronicity is at its best running a store like mine. It's not unusual for a customer to ask for a specific rock that might not be in stock or that I haven't heard of. Within a few days, I will inevitably come across that gemstone through one of my rock dealers. Not only is this great for customer relations, but it also adds another level of awakening to my own path as a gemstone enthusiast. Of course, if I get that gem in the store for my customer, I must have one for my own collection to help me on my life's journey too! This fieldwork has been invaluable. At the time, I didn't realize it would become part of my knowledge base for numerous books and decks.

My first book, *Chakra Awakening: Transform Your Reality Using Crystals, Color, Aromatherapy & the Power of Positive Thought*, is the foundation of the many books and decks that followed, including this one. This book covered many of my interests: crystals, aromatherapy, chakras, and color. Using colors to benefit certain situations was a part of my life even during my banking years; as a bank division manager, I taught my staff courses on how to work with color for personal power and self-development. This knowledge translated beautifully as I transitioned into running my own metaphysical store and authoring many books and decks.

Over the years, I have realized that the world of crystals is a major part of my soul's purpose. It only took a few years for me to realize that my life would be enmeshed with the gemstone kingdom. Using these treasures from the earth is a great way to awaken spiritual consciousness. Working with crystals activates the energy of the chakras, especially when you use them with focused intent. Crystals and a clear intention have gotten me through many tough moments in my life.

The use of gemstones is wide and varied. I see them as beautiful friends from the earth, sparkling with beauty and innate vibrations. Throughout this book, I will share how you can work with crystals to improve your life on all levels: spiritually, physically, mentally, and emotionally. One of my goals for this book is to teach you how to change unconscious influences into conscious intentions using crystals as a tool for self-awareness.

Chapter One

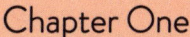

BRINGING CRYSTALS INTO YOUR LIFE
How to Find Them, How to Care for Them, and More

If you have walked into a crystal shop or browsed crystals online, you might have felt drawn to specific stones. This is normal. Trust your gut and choose crystals because you like the way they look; try not to look up their meanings initially. You will naturally be attracted to what you need at any given moment.

You don't need to be a lightworker or a metaphysician to add crystals to your life. Crystals are for everyone! For example, emerald, lapis lazuli, jasper, and carnelian were used in ancient Egyptian amulets; crystal healing is a practice found in Hinduism; and the use of gemstones was mentioned in the Bible. Aaron, the brother of Moses and high priest of the Israelites, was said to have a breastplate with twelve gems: carnelian, chrysolite (probably chrysoberyl), emerald, turquoise, sapphire, amethyst, jacinth, agate, quartz, beryl (probably aquamarine), lapis lazuli, and jasper.

So, no matter who you are or what you believe, you can work with crystals to make changes that will improve your life in the short term and the long term. Pairing gemstones with your intentions can change your life. After all, when you change your mind, you change your life. Make a conscious decision to improve and then use gemstones to stay focused on your intended outcome.

The Short, Sweet Guide to Gemology

This is a very brief gemology lesson to give you some insight into the types of stones.

- *Minerals* are naturally occurring materials containing chemical, physical, and optical parts.
- *Aggregates* consist of a mixture of minerals that can be manually separated.
- *Rocks* are mineral aggregates that contain one or more minerals.
- *Crystals* are minerals that have smooth sides, a point, and edges.

- *Gemstone* is a broad term that includes organic and man-made, inorganic, gemlike materials.
- *Fossils* are the preserved remains of plants, animals, and other living organisms from the past.
- *Quartz* is silicon dioxide that crystallizes and is found in masses. Depending on its color, quartz is found in many forms, including amethyst, citrine, smoky quartz, rose quartz, and rock crystal quartz.
- *Chalcedony* is a family of stones that includes agate and jasper. These stones are composed of tiny or microscopic quartz.
- *Obsidian* is a natural glass formed during the cooling of volcanic lava.
- *Igneous rocks* are solid lava or magma. *Magma* is a liquid rock inside a volcano, and *lava* is the liquid rock (magma) that flows out of a volcano.
- *Metamorphic rocks* are rocks changed by heat, pressure, or other natural means.
- *Sedimentary rocks* are rock types formed by the deposit of material at the earth's surface and within bodies of water.

Although gemological references are made throughout this little book, further gemology information is beyond the scope of

Crystals for Fire Signs

◆

Fire signs' positive attributes are typically creativity, passion, and courage. They are innovative, inspired, spontaneous, and thoughtful. Here are some gemstones that amplify these signs' positive attributes.

ARIES (MARCH 21–APRIL 19): The key phrase is "I am." Mars is Aries' planetary ruler. People born under the sign of Aries are good leaders and great at starting projects, though they might need a bit of extra motivation to finish the job. Orange and red stones support Aries' qualities. **Carnelian**, a stone of creativity, energizes you to take action on your ideas. **Garnet**, a stone of passion and determination, releases procrastination and manifests your desires. **Ruby** is a stone of motivation and inner strength and can get you fired up if you lack enthusiasm.

LEO (JULY 23–AUGUST 22): The key phrase is "I will." The fifth sign, Leo, has the Sun—a light and luminary—as its planetary ruler. Leos like the limelight and have high self-confidence. **Golden topaz** increases courage, amplifies self-esteem, and focuses on positive energy and good thoughts. **Peridot** is the traditional gemstone for Leo and helps you transcend challenges and access your inner strength. The transformative vibration of peridot shifts self-sabotage, jealousy, and impatience. **Sunstone**'s luminosity illuminates the power of your mind to create and attract good fortune. Use it for spiritual magnificence and brilliance as it raises your self-esteem.

SAGITTARIUS (NOVEMBER 22–DECEMBER 21):
The key phrase is "I see." Jupiter, the benevolent planet, is this sign's planetary ruler. Sagittariuses are abstract thinkers and are ready to learn new things; they enjoy traveling to expand their horizons. **Blue topaz**, the traditional gemstone for Sagittarius, is a stone of mental clarity. It brings inspiration, calms emotions, and increases intuitive guidance. **Lapis lazuli** helps you listen to the small voice within and focus on higher knowledge and scholarly subjects. **Sodalite** is a good grounding stone. Use it for focus and meditation, balancing emotions, and releasing anger and frustration. It is also an excellent study aid when learning something new.

this book. The information here is meant to enhance your body, mind, and spirit with conscious attention paired with crystals.

All Shapes and Sizes

Crystals, minerals, and stones come in various shapes and sizes. You can obtain gemstones in their natural state, or you can buy crystals that are tumbled, polished, and/or cut into various geometric configurations.

Rough

Rough stones are a raw form of the mineral found in nature. They have an unpolished appearance. Typically, the color and shine of the stone are muted in its rough form. Rough stones are created by taking a hammer to a larger chunk of rock. The stone will come apart in the direction of its natural cleave. *Cleavage* refers to how a gemstone breaks along a line of weakness or a weakly bonded plane. These rough stones are then sold. Rough chunks are more affordable than, say, a fine specimen. Whereas a rough stone is simply a chunk of rock, a fine specimen is a naturally occurring gem that shows off the rock's natural cleave, cubic shape, druzy (a natural formation of tiny crystals), or cluster formation.

Gemstone clusters grow within the veins of mountains worldwide, and every gemstone cluster is one of a kind. Clusters are a family of points that share a common matrix. The cluster, therefore, represents community connections, starting with a happy family life and learning how to share common ground even though each point/person is unique.

There is sacred geometry within all life, and it is more apparent in raw gemstone specimens. Awareness of a stone's geometry helps delve into the spiritual and metaphysical meanings behind shapes and patterns.

Tumbled

Tumbled stones are rocks that have been polished, rounded, and smoothed. They are the polished versions of rough stones. Tumbled stones are made using a rock tumbler, which incorporates water, grit, and polish. While tumbling enhances the colors and patterns of the stone, this process can take days, weeks, or even months.

Tumbled stones are popular and are found throughout most New Age stores. They are a good option when starting your crystal collection, as tumbled stones and rough, unpolished stones are typically more affordable than other forms.

Shaped

Stones are available as points, palm stones, spheres, worry stones, and in many other shapes, including animals, flowers, bonsai trees, hearts, and pyramids.

A crystal point is easy to hold in your hand, display, or gaze into. Another popular option is the palm stone, which is typically a large oval stone that fits comfortably in the palm of your hand. Many shops sell rocks shaped like spheres, crystal balls, or orbs, which is a stunning way to show off a gemstone. They are pleasant to gaze at during meditation practice because spheres help us connect with the oneness of life. Depending on the density of the stone, they are also beautifully illuminated on a light box. Worry stones are usually about two inches long and one and a half inches wide. They are oval with a thumb-sized indentation. The concave shape is an area that can be rubbed back and forth to calm the mind.

Crystals carved into animal shapes are a great way to introduce the gemstone kingdom to children, though adults are equally attracted to animal shapes and tend to collect specific animals such as owls or cats. Sometimes, you can find a gemstone carved into a rose, a lotus, or another floral shape; these make pretty additions to the home or your desk. Gemstone bonsai trees are a great hostess gift or a nice addition to a home's décor. Gemstone trees come in various stone combinations and sizes and are used for good luck, healing, prosperity, or protection. Heart-shaped gemstones are prolific and popular for heart-centered spiritual development. They make good handheld stones to refocus energy and represent love, friendship, and compassion. Gems shaped

Crystals for Careers in Building

Pyrite crystallizes in the cubic system, representing building blocks and strong foundations, which makes it a perfect pairing for general contractors. Focus on pyrite to strengthen your self-confidence and financial success. Commonly used in electrical wiring, **copper**'s conductive qualities support creative thinking and problem-solving skills; therefore, it is good for electricians. The historic nature of this metal increases your ability to access your creative gifts for substantial monetary gain. **Sardonyx** amplifies your innate invention skills, which supports engineers. Use sardonyx when doing research and developing products or projects.

like pyramids are useful to amplify focus. They have a grounding force, and the point aligns you with your intentions.

You can find gemstones in so many forms. Even if a stone is polished smooth, its inherent geometric pattern is present. The energy is still there, though it has changed. Let yourself be naturally attracted to stones without much thought about the form. It is your intention, paired with the stone you like, that brings your intended goal into reality.

Finding Crystals

Visit a local metaphysical shop or rock shop. You can google "crystal shop near me" to see all your options. When you arrive, see if a staff member will show you around before you start shopping. Start by walking the entire store to see what they carry, making mental notes as you browse. Use your intuition to make your choices. Avoid looking up a crystal's meaning immediately.

Often, metaphysical stores will have shelf-talkers or stone signs describing the main uses of each stone. There may be copies of gemstone books for sale that you could reference to learn about the stone you've chosen. If they have stone signs available, grab one for each rock you pick so you'll remember what you purchased when you get home. Some people like to take photos with the stone sign and crystal next to each other for future reference.

There are also reputable online sources for purchasing gemstones. For example, my store currently offers a weekly Facebook Live event to show off the stones that just arrived. We show them on Facebook Live before they are placed in the showrooms to give our online customers first dibs on the new arrivals. You can find live events on most social media platforms with a little searching. Live events are fun and interactive, and you can usually get a good look at a stone before buying it. Watch a few live events before buying to find reputable sources.

Cleansing Crystals

Once you have purchased a crystal, you should clear it, also known as *cleansing*. There are many clearing techniques for crystals. It is great to have choices depending on the situation or environment.

Water

One of my favorite ways to cleanse crystals is to rinse them under running tap water. It doesn't seem very glamorous or ritualistic to rinse crystals in the kitchen sink, but water is a profound clearing agent that revitalizes the stone's flow.

In my experience, a quick rinse will not affect the integrity of the stones as long as they are dried immediately. However, not all gemstones should be run under water; some are susceptible to water damage. For example, gems that end in -ite

*Crystals and Essential Oils
for Love and Friendship*

Geranium and **rose quartz** pair well for harmonious interactions. Inhale the scent of geranium to find solutions and cooperate with others. Invite compassion, kindness, and loving energy with rose quartz in hand. This duo is perfect for increasing comfort and unconditional love. Rose quartz is a heart chakra stone, and geranium essential oil cancels out negative and angry vibes. Together, this combination uplifts and opens your heart to loving interactions. *Consult a healthcare provider before using geranium if pregnant.*

and others, such as aquamarine, tourmaline, moonstone, lapis lazuli, opal, jasper, and jet. You can go online to learn if your crystal is water safe. Whether or not a crystal is water safe, avoid saltwater baths, which often ruin a stone's finish or polish.

Pulsed Breath

When you don't have access to running water, you can cleanse your crystal using pulsed breath with intention. This is a great method because you don't have to purchase anything, and you can clear a crystal whenever you want, wherever you are.

Marcel Vogel (1917–1991) was a scientist who worked with pulsed breath. In his lifetime, Marcel received over one hundred patents for his inventions. Through scientific experimentation, he discovered that thought can be pulsed within a crystal using the breath. Marcel was instrumental in bridging science and spirituality with his research on quartz crystals.

I had the opportunity to learn from Marcel shortly before he passed; it was an honor to spend time with him in person. He taught me to clear a small quartz crystal using my breath and intention. First, he showed me how to use my dominant hand to roll the crystal clockwise while pressing firmly on each facet. Then, I placed the forefinger and thumb of my dominant hand on one end of the stone and created a cross current by putting the forefinger and thumb of my nondominant hand on the opposite side. I inhaled through my nose while forming the intention to cleanse the crystal, then exhaled forcefully, pulsing my intention into the stone with my breath. Personally, I believe this is the most effective way to clear a crystal, and it can be done anytime and anywhere. A strong and focused intention is crucial to clearing your crystals effectively.

Smoke

Smoke has been used in spiritual practices for millennia because of its ethereal qualities and tendency to rise toward the heavens. A traditional spiritual practice for clearing away negative thoughtforms and vibrations involves using the smoke of burning herbs, typically dried sage. However, sage is not the only option, and since it is overharvested, I recommend choosing another cleansing herb. To smoke cleanse, you will need dried herbs, a lighter, and a dish (such as an abalone shell) to catch or hold the burning embers of your herbs. Using a feather to fan the smoke in the direction you want it to go is valuable and helps sweep away negativity.

MAKING AN HERBAL CLEARING BLEND

Combine the following ingredients in approximately equal proportions: dried eucalyptus, cedar, and lavender. Add a few granules of resins to the mixture; I recommend copal, frankincense, myrrh, and sandalwood. Next, light an incense charcoal and place it in a firesafe pot or bowl. After the charcoal has

Crystals for Careers in Education

Physical training as a profession, which includes physical therapists, Pilates instructors, and yoga instructors, falls in the education category. **Orange calcite** is helpful for physical trainers, as it helps catapult you into new health habits. **Fluorite** has been known as the "genius stone" throughout the ages and is ideal for focus and concentration, which makes it a great match for teachers. **Angelite** is a stone of communication, which is why professors benefit from angelite to help them go within to hear and write their work.

fully ignited, add a pinch of the mixture and use the smoke to clear negative energy.

The Planets

The energy of the sun, the moon, and planetary alignments provides another avenue to recalibrating your gemstones—and yourself. You can put your stones outside to recharge under the full moon or midday sun. The practice can be short and sweet. A simple ten-minute period of mindfulness can connect you and your chosen crystals with the light of the sun. Visualize how the gems and your body are absorbing the healing light for overall well-being. A similar practice can be performed under a full moon. Depending on the size of your collection, I recommend including a few crystals in each energetic connection with the sun, the moon, and planetary configurations.

If you are astrologically savvy, or if you know someone who is, find out when the next significant planetary event will occur, and spend some time outside during that time frame. I recommend choosing a conjunction that only comes around every so often or a specific alignment or configuration of planets. Astrological geometric vibrations are established by the connections between the planets, and they create not only conjunctions but squares, trines, and sextiles. There have been and will be important geometric vibrations from the heavenly bodies, so decide which crystals you want to charge in that specific energy. You can then store them for future use.

Other Stones

Selenite effectively clears and recharges other stones as well as gemstone jewelry. White and red selenite are equally effective. Choose a piece you are drawn to and place it on your altar or dresser for easy access; I recommend using a selenite bowl, log, charging plate, or grid. Place other stones on or around the selenite to absorb its magic.

Blessed Water

You can cleanse your rocks with holy water. You can obtain holy water from fountains in most Catholic churches. Some metaphysical stores sell holy water for three or four dollars; holy water is also available online from eight to thirty dollars. Some rivers or bodies of water are considered blessed; you could gather a bottle of water there and use that instead.

The pulsed breath technique works to charge and bless water. Instead of a stone, hold a bottle or pitcher of water as you pulse the breath through your nose, sending charged blessings into the water.

Essential Oils

As an aromatherapist, I like to use a liquid clearing blend on my crystals. Liquid clearing blends include medical-grade essential

Crystals for Intuition: Clairsentience

Clairsentience is the ability to pick up feelings from people and situations. It's a gut feeling that alerts you to what is good and what is not so good. **Amber** and **black tourmaline** will help you become more aware of and sensitive to the feelings of others. **Moonstone** is beneficial for interpreting what you are feeling while **tiger iron** keeps you grounded and discerning. Use tiger iron to separate others' feelings from your own. These stones will improve your ability to understand and share the feelings of another.

oils, holy water, and other ingredients. They amplify intentions to clear the stone(s), replace negativity with blessings, and enhance well-being.

MAKING A LIQUID CLEARING BLEND

Purchase a two-ounce bottle with a sprayer. Add about two ounces of water to the bottle. Then, put in a few drops of holy water, six drops of sage essential oil, two drops of cedarwood essential oil, and six drops of lavender essential oil. Drop in a tiny clear quartz point. Then, shake, spray, and set your intention to clear your space. You can spray this directly on water safe crystals as well.

Clearing your crystals isn't simply about removing negativity; more importantly, it charges your gems with love, kindness, compassion, and true happiness. No matter what cleansing method you use, the most important ingredients are your thoughts and intentions.

The Power of Intention

I'd like to say more about thoughts and intentions. You need to know what you want to create the life you want. Do you know what you want? It is essential to stop focusing on what you *don't* want in your life, because whatever you focus on becomes your reality. Every conscious and unconscious thought and feeling creates the life you are experiencing right now. This is a fundamental principle—the heart of the universal principle of the law of attraction.

Crystals Amplify Your Intention

Does a crystal create your reality, or is it you? It is you—always you. Every thought, word, feeling, and action you have creates your reality. When paired with a thought or intention, the crystal amplifies what you are creating. So, both you and the crystal are working to create your reality. Pairing crystals with affirmations can help you achieve and maintain a balanced and happy existence. It's all about mindfulness and intention.

Mindfulness

Mindfulness is the state of being conscious or aware of something. True mindfulness is achieved by placing your awareness in the present moment. It is understanding your environment and all the elements within it. Through this observation, you become situationally aware. Examples are watching your surroundings while driving or being conscious of what's happening while walking around a store. Mindfulness is your perception of your environment, what it means to you, and how it affects your happiness and safety. When mindful intention is paired with crystals in daily practice, this helps you start your day with clarity and conscious awareness.

Chapter Two
CRYSTALS ALL DAY LONG

In this chapter, you will learn about working with crystals in your daily life at various times of the day and night. There are many choices for incorporating crystals into your daily routine to make life more joyful, productive, and positive.

Morning Essentials

While having a morning routine is a common thing, each routine is quite different and personal. In my life, I devote about three days to writing and household stuff; the other days, I'm focused on getting to work and running my shop. I gravitate to some stones while writing and to others to get into the groove of merchandising and working with customers. The stones on my writing desk are elestial quartz, sodalite, carnelian, fluorite, rose quartz, and many other types of quartz crystals. The stones at the desk in my office are a rose quartz Ganesha, a tall rose quartz standing point, a chrysoprase heart, and tumbled stones like prasiolite and purpurite. Think about the components of your days to integrate crystals into your own routine.

Start the morning thinking about how you want your day to go. Quiet your mind and contemplate the upcoming day. I recommend building in ten minutes of quiet each morning. Pick a crystal or two to help with contemplation, meditation, and visualization; clear quartz is good for gaining mental clarity and amplifying the day's intentions. Jot down some thoughts, goals, and intentions. Become aware of anything that might be blocking your happiness, then release it. Refocus on what you want to experience for the day. The morning is a time for self-care, and chrysoprase pairs well with taking good care of yourself.

Pick up your journal and an amethyst to write down impressions from dreams. Be conscious of ideas that have come into your consciousness. Journal for a few moments. You can refer to these thoughts later or before going to sleep that night to determine if there is something you want to dream about or process during your sleepy time.

Crystals for Intuition: Claircognizance

Claircognizance is the ability to know something intuitively. This knowing is beyond logical explanation. An example of claircognizance would be someone asking, "How do you know that?" and being told, "I don't know how I know, but I know!" **Amethyst, clear quartz, Herkimer diamond, scolecite,** and **selenite** are stones that activate higher intuition and connection with divine consciousness. **Celestite** calms incessant mental chatter, which helps with being able to pay attention to intuitive knowing.

Bring orange calcite and selenite for muscular strength when heading out for a morning walk or going to the gym. Garnet and ruby are helpful for endurance. Chalcopyrite supports you when you are engaging in strength training, especially when this training involves outdoor activities. Whether you are practicing Pilates, doing yoga, running, muscle training, or the like, fluorite is a great companion to help you stay on course with your fitness plan; use this "focus stone" to help you maintain discipline.

At breakfast, consider apatite, malachite, peridot, and yellow jasper your allies for mindful eating. Keeping a few tumbled stones in a dish in the kitchen or the breakfast area will help you align with mindful eating when you see them. These crystals aid with digestion. Keep them nearby to establish conscious support for the optimal function of the gallbladder, liver, pancreas, and spleen. Additionally, magnesite is helpful for muscle relaxation, healthy evacuation of the large intestines, and ease of food absorption and digestion.

The Stone of the Day

Wearing crystals is fashionable and fun. As you get dressed, choose a stone of the day and pair it with positive thoughts and feelings. You can decide which stone (or stones) to use based on your mood, or you can wait until you've chosen the color of your outfit. Notice what color comes to mind when you think about your outfit for the day, then take a moment to contemplate why you are attracted to that specific color. You are naturally drawn to what you need. This practice helps with self-knowledge and mindfulness.

Once you have a color in mind, choose a matching gemstone bracelet, a pendant and earrings, or put the stone of the day in tumbled form in your pocket, bra, or carry bag. Think about all the positive benefits of the stone you chose. Every time you see it, touch it, or think of it, bring that stone's positive intentions and purposes to mind. I have provided information about the most popular rocks (based on my experiences as a retailer and author) throughout this book.

Out the Door

Incorporate crystals into your morning commute. If you drive to work, keeping a clear quartz crystal in your car will maintain your intention of staying focused and mentally alert while driving. If you walk or bike to work, selenite and orange calcite are good stones for muscle and tendon support. Carrying a small tumbled stone in your pocket, backpack, or bra is an easy way to keep one with you. If you take the bus, subway, or train, wear a gemstone bracelet or necklace to keep the space around you sacred and clear. When immersed in public transportation, you could pick up other people's thoughts and feelings. Amber, amethyst, and black tourmaline are good choices to keep negativity at bay and to protect your personal

Crystals for Earth Signs

People born under an earth sign are honest, reliable, practical, and grounded. They persevere and maintain focus. Here are some gemstones that amplify these signs' positive attributes.

TAURUS (APRIL 20–MAY 20): The key phrase is "I have." Venus is this sign's planetary ruler. Tauruses are determined and a stabilizing force. **Emerald**, the green variety of beryl, grounds you with spiritual calmness and awakens inner wisdom. It is a stone of healing, prosperity, and financial success. **Green tourmaline** aligns you with heart-centered awareness and helps attract compassion. Use it to achieve business success and to attract ethical, loyal friends and business associates. **Hematite** has a grounding effect, removes scattered energy, and brings focused determination. It repels negative thoughts and amplifies feelings of calmness and well-being.

VIRGO (AUGUST 23–SEPTEMBER 22): The key phrase is "I analyze." Virgo's ruling planet is Mercury. Detail-oriented Virgos have **sapphire**

as their traditional birthstone. Use this blue gem to align with wisdom and truth. Sapphire supports altruism, wise leadership, and Virgo's innate reliability, perfectionism, and intelligence. **Green calcite**, a stone of transformation, opens the heart center, encouraging compassion, tolerance, and understanding. It promotes the healthy function of the digestive organs and the integration of life's challenges. **Kyanite**, a stone of balance and alignment, calms emotions and reduces anger and frustration.

CAPRICORN (DECEMBER 22–JANUARY 19): The key phrase is "I use." Capricorn's ruling planet is Saturn. Capricorns have good potential for acquiring wealth and success. **Garnet** is a traditional birthstone that activates passion and determination. Use garnet to stay on course to manifest your intentions. **Ruby** encourages taking action to create your desired reality. Use both gems to amplify wealth and overall success in all aspects of life. **Pyrite**'s block-like structure resonates with Capricorn's strong foundation. All three stones will help you take the action required to develop and manifest.

space. Using crystals is a great way to draw the proverbial line of demarcation: This is my space, and that is your space.

Mid-Morning Motivators

With clear quartz in hand or on your desk, make to-do lists. Keep the clear quartz nearby and pick it up throughout the day to help you stay focused. You can also keep Herkimer diamonds nearby. These are doubly terminated quartz crystals that promote clarity and energetic action. Herkimer diamonds sharpen your focus and mental ability, and they awaken the desire to learn new things.

Use red jasper for steadfast action toward the goals you've included on your to-do list. This crystal also supports following through and taking the necessary steps to see a project to fruition. Red jasper can be used to develop your strength and improve your vital life force, so this stone is useful for restoring, regenerating, and rejuvenating your passion.

Pyrite, the stone of financial abundance, is a good stone to have nearby when working toward goals involving financial success or prosperity. Both pyrite and citrine are beneficial when you need to increase confidence and believe in your ability to increase monetary wealth. Other powerful stones for motivation are garnet, red tiger's eye, rutilated quartz, and ruby.

Having crystals around will improve the energy of your space. I recommend leaving a bowl of crystals around your workspace to gaze at and pick up when you are drawn to. Think about why you might be attracted to that specific crystal at that time.

Afternoon Pick-Me-Up

Let's talk about some gemstones that help to energize and motivate. Get over the afternoon slump with crystals like carnelian, garnet, ruby, red jasper, clear quartz, Herkimer diamond, rutilated quartz, and sunstone.

Carnelian is a stone of creativity and motivation. This beautiful orange chalcedony is sure to uplift and inspire. Carnelian aids in creating new ideas and completing projects. I have a piece of carnelian on my writing desk that I gaze at when I need to complete an article or a book submission.

Garnet and ruby have similar energetic imprints that bring passion and blessings. Wear them as jewelry to stay energized all day, as they amplify energy and vital life force. Let these stones bring more vim and vigor to your afternoon.

The key phrase I use to sum up the energy of red jasper is "manifesto presto," which refers to its ability to make things happen. Use this stone to manifest your goals and intentions.

With its full spectrum of light, clear quartz enhances and amplifies your good intentions. Use it to gain clarity and direction. Similarly, Herkimer diamonds are clear quartz crystals mined in Herkimer, New York, and their natural formation mimics diamonds. Even the smallest Herkimer diamonds can energize your mind and body to move forward and stay alert.

Rutilated quartz contains long, thin, hairlike minerals composed of titanium dioxide that promote fine-tuned thinking. Work with this crystal to boost your courage, energy, and self-esteem. Visualize your energy levels improving with this stone in hand.

Sunstone amplifies your vital life force. Gaze at the sunstone's luminosity with positive thoughts to promote passionate action and motivation. The orange colors of platy copper, goethite, and hematite within sunstone bring fortitude and self-confidence.

Chilling for the Evening

Evening is the time to pause for a mindful moment. Still your mind as you check in with yourself about how you handled everything throughout the day. Ask yourself if there were any situations that you would handle differently the next time. This is a great time to pick up your journal and some gemstones for personal development and self-improvement. Hold the recommended stones or keep them nearby while you journal or contemplate.

Crystals like moonstones can be used to help with self-observation. *Self-observation* is the act of observing one's behaviors, reactions, and actions as an interested, objective observer—without judgment. Moonstone is a crystal of reflection, so gaze at the stone as you look within for self-improvement and spiritual growth. Look at the shimmer in the stone, known as *adularescence*. Window clear quartz crystals have a perfect diamond-shaped face, usually a seventh facet, and are beneficial for open-eyed contemplation. Stare at the diamond-shaped face on the point as you empty your mind of its regular chatter. This type of clear quartz helps you observe your thoughts, patterns, and behaviors so you can release those that are not aligned with higher consciousness.

If the evenings are when you find yourself gravitating toward a habit that isn't the best for you, there are crystals that can help with that. Are you a late-night overeater, or do you have a tendency to drink a bit too much alcohol in the evening? You are not alone, and you *can* overcome these habits. Blue and teal stones like sodalite, apatite, and chrysocolla bring calmness and help release the urge to overeat and other negative habits. Amethyst is notorious for being the sobriety stone, so keep amethyst nearby to maintain sobriety; it's also good prep for sleeping and dreaming.

Crystal Alignments for Self-Healing

A crystal alignment, also known as the laying on of stones, involves placing gemstones and crystals on and around the body to restore balance. This is a great evening practice after a stressful day.

Collect one or three stones for each of the seven chakras (either seven or twenty-one crystals total). Once you have gathered your selected stones, lie down and place them on your body. Set the rocks on top of the corresponding chakras. Then, relax and meditate as the stones support your inner voyage. If arranging the stones on yourself is too difficult, you can ask a friend or family member to place the stones as you relax.

Sleepy Time Crystals

When it is time to lower the lights and relax into deep rest, set the stage as you turn down the bed. Spray some essential oil blends to support sweet dreams and a good night's sleep. Chamomile and lavender encourage peaceful sleep and relax the body, mind, and spirit.

Amethyst, a purple-colored quartz, is one of the best stones for dreaming and restful sleep. Use amethyst to prevent nightmares, encourage dream recall, and ensure a deep and restful sleep. Ametrine (a combination of amethyst and citrine), amethyst clusters and cathedrals, chevron amethyst, and tumbled stones and points all work well.

Hematite is useful for calming and relaxing because it shifts negative feelings and emotional challenges. Keeping hematite near you while you sleep can help prevent muscle cramping, balance the nervous system, and relieve insomnia. It's the perfect rock to encourage deep rest. If all you have is rough hematite,

Crystals for Careers in Entertainment

♦

The vibrant colors of **peacock copper** exemplify an actor's energy. Let peacock copper remind you to use your creative energy and show your brilliance. **Aragonite** motivates you to move and increases flexibility, making it the ultimate gem for dancers. Use aragonite while improving the health of your bones, muscles, and overall body. **Blue calcite** helps performers tap into their voice and their communication skills.

Creating a Crystal Garden Wheel

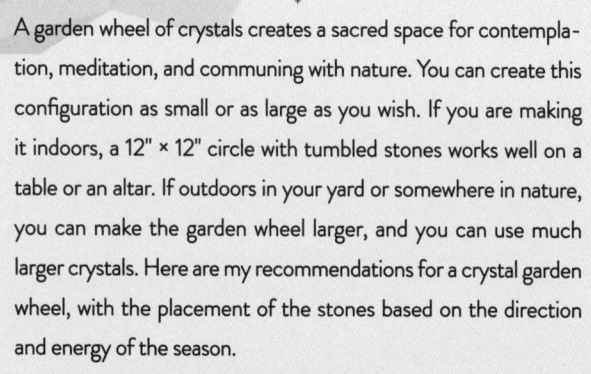

◆

A garden wheel of crystals creates a sacred space for contemplation, meditation, and communing with nature. You can create this configuration as small or as large as you wish. If you are making it indoors, a 12" × 12" circle with tumbled stones works well on a table or an altar. If outdoors in your yard or somewhere in nature, you can make the garden wheel larger, and you can use much larger crystals. Here are my recommendations for a crystal garden wheel, with the placement of the stones based on the direction and energy of the season.

In the east, place a piece of **clear quartz** for clarity, illumination, and the ability to see life from a greater perspective. In the southeast, **green moss agate** aligns you with nature and growth. In the south, **carnelian** represents the sun, and the light shines brightly to fire up your energy. In the southwest, **amethyst** can be placed to gain clarity on dreams and prepare for going within to understand situations. In the west, place **black obsidian**. Use black obsidian to delve into your inner thoughts and feelings; it is a potent stone for manifestation with creative visualization. In the northwest, use **citrine** to become a conscious creator of your own fate. Inner strength and courage can be cultivated at this point. In the north, **elestial quartz** attunes your awareness to the ancestors' wisdom. Stare at the formation within the elestial quartz and on the surface as you relax and receive inspiration from your ancestors and higher wisdom. In the northeast, **selenite** represents the return of the light.

keep the stone on your nightstand; if you have tumbled hematite, go ahead and put it in your pillowcase.

Sleep affects your overall health and every system of your body. Getting adequate sleep supports healthy brain function and physical health. I recommend creating a crystal grid in your bedroom for sound sleep, to feel safe, and for pleasant dreams.

Crystal Grids

A crystal grid is a formation of gemstones arranged in or around a person, place, or thing, sometimes in a geometric pattern, to amplify an intention. Establish a crystal grid in your bedroom, including your adjoining bathroom if you have one.

Place gems around the room, like on top of a shelf or dresser, on the windowsill, between the mattress and the box springs, and on the nightstand. As you place the stones with conscious intention, identify your goals and visualize your ideal outcome as if it has already become a reality. You could also place gemstones in such a way that they would create a geometric formation, like a triangle, if you were to "connect the dots" between the crystals in your space. Visualize and imagine that these crystals are connecting like a dot puzzle, establishing a light grid around you and your sleeping quarters.

There are many options for a crystal grid designed to help with sleep. A selenite lamp, selenite logs, or selenite wands can amplify the vibrations of love and light in your space, bringing protection, healing, and peace to you and your surroundings. The calming, heavenly shades of blue calcite relieve stress and bring a blanket of peaceful energy. Add rose quartz for comfort and love. Include black tourmaline, fluorite, and shungite to deflect harmful electromagnetic frequencies from your mobile phone, tablet, and television. I have all of these stones and more in my bedroom!

Crystal grids can be customized for any intention. For example, smoky quartz maintains protective energy, as do black tourmaline, black obsidian, and jet. Include clear quartz points and selenite wands or discs to amplify light and good vibes. Amethyst transforms unwanted habits, and rose quartz invites more love and compassion. Choose your stones based on what you like to look at and the gemstones' qualities.

You can also purchase geometric crystal grid boards or create your own. Premade crystal grid boards make it easier to create a grid of crystals because the geometric grid lines are in place. Grid boards are portable and take up very little space. Place small stones on each point of the grid while you focus on your intention. See Crystals for Crystal Grids (page 77) for more ideas.

Chapter Three

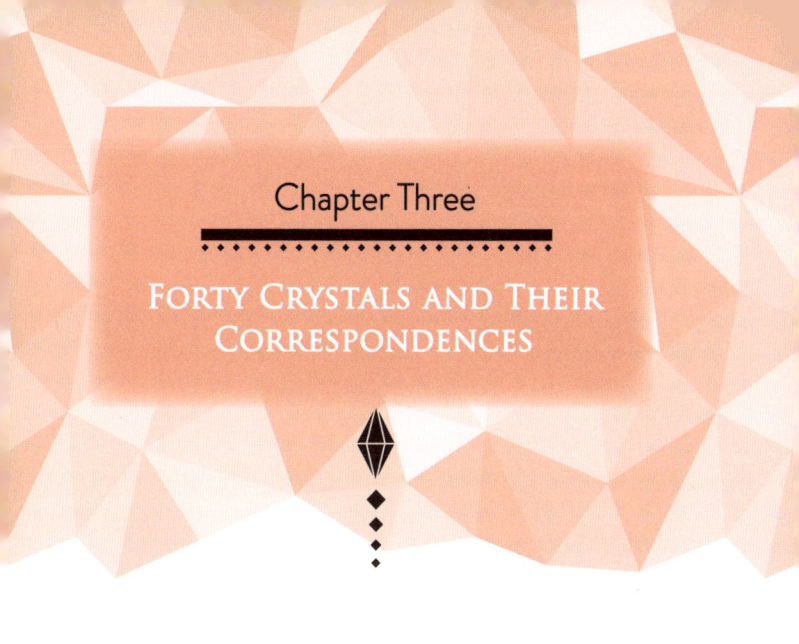

Forty Crystals and Their Correspondences

Each crystal has numerous correspondences, from the chakras to the elements and more. The vibration of the stone's color, the mineral contents, and how it is found in the earth all contribute to its energetic vibration. In this chapter, I have focused on forty stones that are easy to find at your local rock shop or metaphysical store. Keep in mind that the gemstones in this chapter are just a starting point—there are thousands of gems to choose from! The crystals you are naturally drawn to are likely the crystals you need.

Before we dive in, I would like to expand on some of the correspondences that will be explored for each crystal in this chapter.

Divinatory Meanings

Crystals are helpful for divination. You can use your collection of crystals to get to know yourself better and to navigate life's challenges. When you are uncertain about what to do, use this book like a "magic book." Think about a question, open to this part of the book, and read the first divinatory meaning you see. You can also pick a stone you are attracted to and read the divinatory meaning for insight and inspiration. The oracular value of crystals is immense. Using crystals for divination will give you a better understanding of yourself and your situation based on the meaning of your chosen gemstones. Use these sparkling treasures to live a more fulfilling life.

Color and the Chakras

The nature of color is universal. Color affects our psychological responses, whether or not we are aware of that. Because color can influence mood and impact behavior, the colors we wear and the colors in the environment have a very specific effect. Using crystals, with their array of vibrant colors, has an impact that is subtle yet obvious. Crystals can evoke feelings ranging from peace, love, and warmth to agitation, frustration, and anger. Oftentimes, these feelings are influenced by the color of the crystal.

For example, red is great for amplifying motivation, action, and passion, but too much red when you feel agitated or angry isn't the best idea. Instead, use red's complementary color, green, to restore balance and peace. A complementary color is the color directly opposite on the color wheel. You could also incorporate the color blue, which calms inflammation and agitation. If you feel agitated or angry, carrying or wearing blue and green crystals serves as a reminder to refocus, breathe, and find harmony within.

In this chapter, I have shared the corresponding chakra(s) for each stone. Color is a part of the chakra system, and the use of colorful crystals can bring balance to the chakras. There are two ways crystals can help balance the chakras: either by incorporating the color that corresponds with that chakra, or by incorporating its complementary color. One easy way to do this is by keeping corresponding gemstones nearby during color meditations.

Use the crystals listed in this book as a guide for color meditation and chakra balancing. Utilizing colors, crystals, and the chakras can bring focus, balance, and grounding.

Elements

Each crystal is associated with one of the four elements: fire, air, earth, or water. The fire element denotes courage, passion,

46

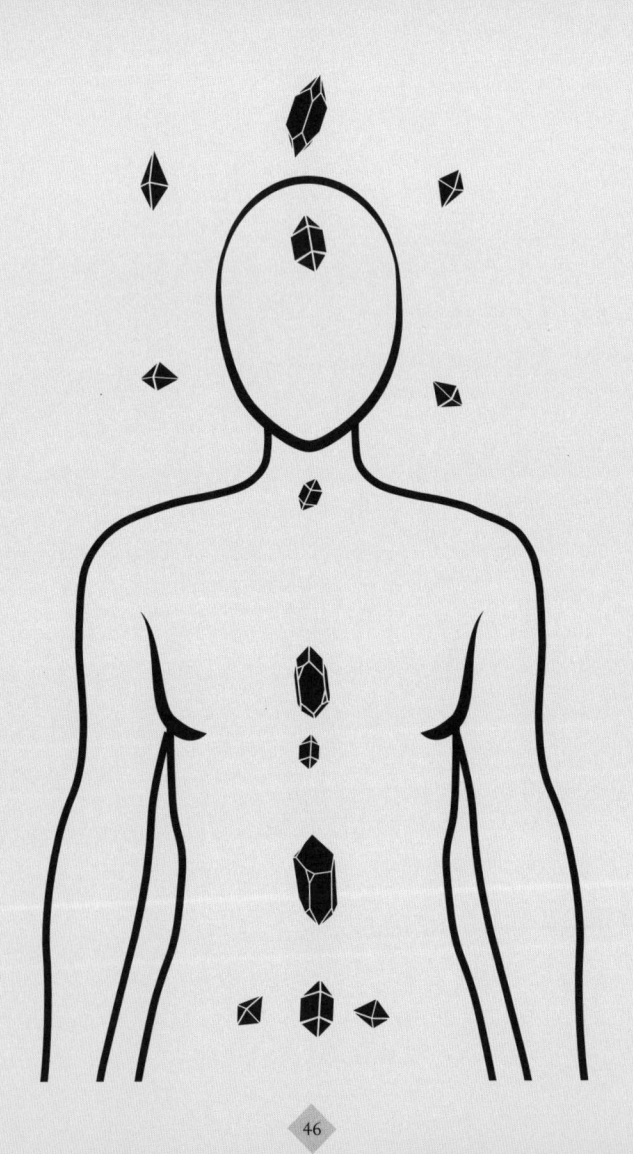

Crystals for a Chakra Alignment

A chakra-balancing crystal alignment, also known as the *laying on of stones*, balances the chakra system. Put crystals on and around the body on the chakras and key energy points such as the palms of your hands and the soles of your feet. Place the crystals with a focused intention to balance the body's energy centers; this can be done while listening to a guided imagery meditation or in complete silence. You can perform a crystal alignment on yourself or on others. Place gemstones on each of the seven chakras based on the corresponding chakra color. Here is one version: Place **clear quartz** above the crown of the head, an **amethyst** on the center of the forehead for the third eye chakra, **angelite** on the throat, **green aventurine** on the center of the chest for the heart chakra, **citrine** on the solar plexus, **carnelian** on the belly for the sacral chakra, and **black tourmaline** by the knees or soles of the feet for the root chakra.

boldness, and enthusiasm. The air element brings the vibration of communication, intellect, and friendliness. The element of earth is a grounding force that brings reliability and protection. The element of water is the vibration of emotions, intuition, and sensitivity. Understanding the element(s) of a crystal gives you more information about that stone.

Crystal Pairings

There are many ways to amplify a crystal's power. So far, I have talked about matching a crystal with a positive thought, affirmation, or intention. In this chapter, you will learn how to pair crystals with essential oils, herbal remedies, animal allies, archangels, angels, and saints.

Bach Flower Remedies

I have included Bach Flower Remedies as an additional tool for working with gemstones to amplify their energy. In the 1930s, Dr. Edward Bach discovered these gentle, vibrational essences, now used worldwide. These liquid essences restore harmony between the soul and the mind. They are created from the essence of plants, flowers, trees, and bushes. Many people believe that Bach Flower Remedies allow the body to fight disease and reduce stress while transforming negative attitudes and beliefs. Dr. Bach wrote, "Disease of the body itself is nothing but the result of the disharmony between soul and mind.

Remove the disharmony, and we regain harmony between soul and mind, and the body is once more perfect in all its parts."[1] I personally have found Bach Flower Remedies' vibrational healing beneficial for mental and emotional challenges that ultimately affected my physical well-being.

Bach Flower Remedies are usually taken internally; include a drop in a bottle of drinking water. You could also add Bach Flower Remedies to a liquid clearing blend: Include the essence in a blend with essential oils and water, then spray it around you and your space. The use of Bach Flower Remedies requires no training; all that is required is an understanding of how they affect us mentally and emotionally.

There are thirty-eight Bach Flower Remedies, each associated with various feelings. Use flower essences during challenging times, when negative feelings arise, or when you feel exhausted to restore balance before physical symptoms appear. I recommend you do your own research to discover which essence is best for your situation instead of asking someone else. Pamphlets, online quizzes, and other guides can help you determine which essence (or series of essences) is best for you.

---

1. Roser Camats Falip, "Dr. Edward Bach," Bach Flower Therapy, accessed September 9, 2024, https://www.bachflowertherapy.us/1-dr-edward-bach.html.

chapter three

Angels, Archangels, and Saints

In this chapter, I sometimes pair gemstones with angels, archangels, and saints in the Pairs Well With section. These spiritual beings can support you in your work with crystals and gemstones. My approach to working with angels, archangels, and saints is metaphysical and spiritual rather than religious. A variety of spiritual philosophies and cultures have experiences and connections with angels, archangels, and saints who have helped teach humankind. You can manifest help from these spiritual beings by calling on them when you feel afraid or need guidance.

Animal Allies

As you read over the meanings and uses of crystals, you will have the opportunity to grasp the interrelatedness of all life on Earth. Teachings from nature, plants, and animals can add another element to a spiritually rich life. Occasionally, I will pair a crystal with a certain animal ally in the Pairs Well With section.

In general, working with animal allies can help you better understand yourself and all life forms. The characteristics of animals—from birds and insects to mammals, fish, and reptiles—provide lessons for life experiences. Animal medicine is a powerful signpost for self-knowledge and for clarity on life's challenges. For example, if a specific animal shows up in your life repetitively or in some out-of-the-ordinary way, it is time to pay attention to the message that nature is bringing you.

Similarly, matching gemstone teachings with animal allies provides you with an even deeper understanding and a life filled with "aha" moments. The spiritual fulfillment you seek is available to you in many ways, and this path of working with gemstones and animal medicine is just one of many.

Note

This section tells you what the stone looks like, the forms it can be found in, and whether or not it is water safe.

Crystals for Careers in Finance

Citrine boosts mental clarity, which makes it an ideal stone for accountants. Work with citrine when you handle your finances or anything mathematical. **Emerald** represents wealth and is a perfect ally for bankers. **Jade** is a highly prized mineral that brings prosperity and is good luck for brokers; it amplifies and symbolizes great wealth. **Pyrite** and **galena** are grounding stones that are helpful for keeping a strong foundation in any business.

Crystals for Channeling and Connecting to the Akashic Records

♦

Channeling quartz is a type of clear quartz point that adds another layer of connection to the Divine. It has a seven-sided face and a three-sided face on the crystal's termination. Use the seven-three vibration for divinely inspired writing, artwork, or another creative venture. This stone is an instrument to channel wisdom and knowledge. **Elestial quartz** is a quartz with multiple terminations, etchings, inclusions, and extrusions, creating a skeletal look. This form of quartz has many geometrical markings. Legend says it was brought through the ethers from the heavenly realm. Gaze at the triangular configurations and markings to tap into information from higher realms. **Lapis lazuli** offers the vibrations of peace and harmony. This third eye chakra stone connects you to intuition, knowing, and visions. Gaze at lapis lazuli to tap into your internal guidance system. **Record keeper quartz** is a quartz point with naturally forming triangular etchings on one or more of the faces of the crystal. Gaze into the etchings and geometric formations while allowing for inspiration to come to you.

Amethyst

chapter three

Amethyst is the stone of transformation. Use the purple glow of amethyst to surround yourself with the transformative ability to change unwanted situations. Amethyst can bring good dreams and chase away nightmares. When things aren't going your way and the road appears blocked, take an amethyst in your hand and establish a clear vision. Envision what needs to be removed or transmuted and focus on the ultimate positive outcome. Amethyst's purple energy gives you the strength and power to make the necessary changes. It stimulates clear seeing and your third eye. You can receive intuitive insights to help you daily through your spiritual connection with the Divine.

> **DIVINATORY MEANING:** Dreams bring realizations through symbols and metaphors. You have the ability to transform your reality using the spiritual guidance you receive. Take the time to imagine your new reality and daydream it into being. A challenge is currently being transformed and transmuted into something powerful.

CHAKRA(S): Crown, third eye

ELEMENT(S): Air

PAIRS WELL WITH: Lavender flowers and essential oils are good matches for amethyst. Its transformational qualities include relieving aching muscles, soothing the emotional body, and improving sleep. Include other stones like charoite, citrine, and sugilite to increase its power. State a positive affirmation like "It is easy for me to transform and transmute challenging situations."

NOTES: Amethyst is a purple quartz crystal. It is available in tumbled stones, points, clusters, and cathedrals. This stone is water safe.

Ametrine

chapter three

Ametrine is a bicolor quartz made of amethyst and citrine. The complementary colors of purple and yellow connect the crown and solar plexus chakras to facilitate connection with higher spiritual wisdom. Use the power of amethyst to transmute negativity and the power of citrine to improve confidence. This stone helps release negative hooks to your emotions and encourages being discerning with the people you let into your life. It alleviates headaches and can be used to rid oneself of digestive challenges. Work with ametrine to let go of unhealthy habits or addictions like smoking, drinking, doing drugs, and overeating.

> **DIVINATORY MEANING:** It's time to release that habit or addiction that holds you back from being all that you can be. Perhaps there is a friendship or relationship that you should step away from. Take action to make the changes to be empowered. Shine your light and live your best life!
>
> **CHAKRA(S):** Crown, third eye, solar plexus
>
> **ELEMENT(S):** Air
>
> **PAIRS WELL WITH:** Ametrine pairs well with smoky quartz and clary sage essential oil. Inhale clary sage to help you remain calm while making necessary lifestyle changes. Include *Walnut* Bach Flower Remedy when

changing from one way of being to another, like when healing an addiction or adjusting your mindset. State an affirmation like "I remain grounded and focused even when the world around me is changing."

NOTES: Ametrine is a bicolor stone displaying the shades purple and yellow. These complementary colors bring balance during challenging situations. This stone is water safe.

Crystals for Air Signs

◆

Air signs are thinkers and analyzers. They generate ideas. Their objective nature allows them to consider various perspectives before deciding or taking action. Here are some gemstones that amplify these signs' positive attributes.

GEMINI (MAY 21–JUNE 21): The key phrase is "I think." Mercury, planetary ruler of Gemini, is associated with communication and thought processes. **Copper** is perfect for Gemini's mercurial nature due to its conductive qualities that benefit communication skills, creating clear messages and receiving inspiration. **Fluorite**, the genius stone, helps you realize you are smart enough and supports clear thinking in both simple and complex situations. It's also been known to help deflect electromagnetic frequencies. **Labradorite**, an excellent gem for reflection, is beneficial for visualizing and realizing the answers to whatever you are searching for. Use it to stay focused on your intentions.

LIBRA (SEPTEMBER 23–OCTOBER 23): The key phrase is "I balance." Libra, ruled by the planet Venus, is associated with balance and partnerships. **Morganite**, the pink variety of beryl, helps you manifest what is best right now and is a great stone for gratitude practices. **Opal**, one of the traditional gemstones for Libra, adds energy to the power of foresight and prophecy, helps maintain emotional balance, and heals hurt feelings. **Rose quartz** adds the vibration of love to all of life's situations. Use it to attract and support faithful friends and partners. It's a good crystal for attracting your soul mate.

AQUARIUS (JANUARY 20–FEBRUARY 18): The key phrase is "I know." Aquarius's ruling planets are Uranus and Saturn, and this sign is associated with large groups, humanitarian efforts, hopes, wishes, and dreams. Aquarians seek spiritual knowledge and are intelligent. **Amber**, one of the traditional birthstones for Aquarius, is a fossilized tree resin that helps maintain healthy boundaries in all areas of life. **Amethyst**, the gem for February birthdays, is the stone for dreaming and transforming your reality to achieve your goals. **Blue calcite**'s calming energy supports focusing on spiritual and metaphysical pursuits. Use blue calcite to deal with unexpected changes and to embrace your inherent spiritual gifts.

Angelite

chapter three

Angelite is your ally when you feel misunderstood or like people aren't listening to you. It's also helpful when you feel timid about speaking the truth. Angelite is a great gem for communicating with the angels. Use it to open yourself up to receiving guidance and messages from the Divine. This stone of communication also helps you become a better listener. Keep it nearby to align with divine timing to be at the right place, at the right time, with the right people. Its calming blue color is also a good support for writing and creating music.

DIVINATORY MEANING: Quiet your mind and listen. You are intuitive and receive messages from the angels. Accept their guidance and notice symbolic messages in your surroundings. You have great timing. Trust yourself. You are eloquent, and people listen to you when you talk.

CHAKRA(S): Throat

ELEMENT(S): Air, water

PAIRS WELL WITH: Add some amazonite and blue lace agate to increase communication effectiveness. Use an aromatherapeutic mist like eucalyptus to use your olfactory senses to improve the balance of your throat chakra. Invite your Guardian Angel to help you to interpret signs and messages from the Divine. Say, "I feel calm and at peace as angels orchestrate my life."

NOTES: Angelite is a pastel blue stone with a white center or flecks of white. This stone is not water safe.

Aquamarine

chapter three

Aquamarine, a blue-green beryl, is an excellent tool for telepathic communication with all life, especially sea creatures. This semiprecious gem is also beneficial for connecting with animal and plant life. On an emotional level, aquamarine can help restore emotional balance. Its calming blue color encourages compassionately accepting the truth and relieves negative energy from conversations with others as well as your own internal dialogue. Use aquamarine for inspiration when writing or developing an artistic creation.

> **DIVINATORY MEANING:** Spend time by a body of water or enjoy a bath. Wash away negative emotions. Let go of replaying conversations that have upset you. Take a moment to let yourself cry—get those watery emotions out of your system to regain emotional balance. Open your mind to sending and receiving telepathic communication to make your life easier.

CHAKRA(S): Throat

ELEMENT(S): Water

PAIRS WELL WITH: Throat chakra stones like angelite and blue lace agate increase the benefits of working with aquamarine; they help you get in touch with your communication skills and telepathic abilities. Connect with water creatures and animal allies such as Frog, Sandpiper, Seagull, and Starfish to regain emotional balance. Amplify good thoughts with aquamarine in hand: "My emotions are balanced. Positive energy supports me in every way."

NOTES: Aquamarine is a beryl mineral that comes in shades of pastel blue and light green. This stone is water safe but can become damaged if submerged for extended periods of time.

Crystals for Connecting with Angels and Archangels

To connect with your Guardian Angel, use **blue lace agate** to help awaken the vibration of divine protection. Believe and know you are never alone. Use **lapis lazuli** to call on Archangel Michael for safety and protection. Michael is dedicated to removing fears and bringing feelings of comfort and safety. Archangel Raphael, the angel of healing, aligns with **emerald**, which amplifies healing on all levels: mentally, emotionally, and spiritually. Archangel Gabriel and **blue sapphire** are a great vibrational match for communication, honesty, integrity, and loyalty. Gabriel is a messenger archangel, the Angel of the Annunciation, well-known for announcing Jesus's birth. Archangel Uriel is associated with thunder and lightning, an energy of enlightenment, sudden realizations, and ideas. **Sunstone** matches Uriel's light and connection with natural phenomena.

Crystals for Careers in Justice

◆

Amazonite is the stone of truth and supports the role of a judge. Use this blue stone to determine the facts. Amazonite will then help you speak graciously and diplomatically. **Hiddenite**, a lawyer's ally, helps maintain an even-keeled and grounded demeanor. Use it to clarify what is happening to determine the best outcome for all concerned. **Black tourmaline** is my go-to stone for safety and protection and is a perfect match for law enforcement personnel.

Black Obsidian

chapter three

Black obsidian is natural glass formed during the cooling of volcanic lava. It's a perfect stone for dealing with emotions buried deep in your consciousness. Sometimes, these emotions can broadcast unconscious messages that perpetuate negative situations. This stone supports you in deflecting negativity. Use this stone to put an end to habits that you don't want to experience anymore. Keep a black obsidian nearby to ground you and maintain focus. Black obsidian is an ally if you tend to be easily distracted. You can also use black obsidian to explore spiritual dreaming and visions.

> **DIVINATORY MEANING:** Quiet reflection will uncover what you need to peel away the layers of your feelings and transform your emotions. Take the steps necessary to clear out damaging vibes. Travel deep within, and uncoil the layers of your consciousness so they can guide you to grow through perceived challenges.

CHAKRA(S): Root

ELEMENT(S): Fire

PAIRS WELL WITH: Black obsidian is a vibrational match with the animal ally Snake. Snake helps you become more aware of the parts of you that need healing. The transformative power of Snake supports you when you need to go beneath surface emotions or perceptions. Use the power of scent to set the energy for your transformational process: Palo santo essential oil helps you recognize the energetic connections between yourself and others; it also clears negative mental energy associated with jealousy, self-doubt, and unnecessary mental chatter.

NOTES: Black obsidian sometimes displays a golden or silver sheen, bubbles formed when the volcanic lava was cooling. This stone is water safe.

Black Onyx

chapter three

Black onyx, the black form of chalcedony, is a grounding tool in everyday life. Use this crystal to get clarity and stay focused in the moment. Black onyx helps improve mindfulness, so it is a good stone to keep on your desk or workspace. It can help you achieve focused awareness with its calming and peaceful vibrations. When you have black onyx in hand, it is protective and helps you avoid destructive habits and responses. Use this stone for mindful self-observation and personal improvement. Black onyx also supports you during the grieving process and deflects negativity.

DIVINATORY MEANING: Use your entrepreneurial spirit to improve your confidence and endurance in a successful career. Stay focused on financial goals to achieve success. Maintain persistence and determination, combined with empathy and kindness. Recognize and accept your sadness, and allow yourself to grieve the losses of your past.

CHAKRA(S): Root

ELEMENT(S): Earth

PAIRS WELL WITH: Golden sheen, rainbow, and snowflake obsidian are excellent tools to dredge up emotions buried deep within you. Ravensara essential oil helps clear your consciousness, allowing you to receive higher levels of prophetic dreaming or messages from a deeper part of yourself. Bach Flower Remedies like *Agrimony*, *Chest-*

nut Bud, and *White Chestnut* support learning from repetitive mistakes. Affirm a positive thought like "I am always safe and protected."

NOTES: The onyx referred to in this entry is black, and it is used for protection and strength. However, onyx comes in other colors like green, associated with the heart chakra; red and white, associated with the sacral and root chakras; and brown and white, called *sardonyx*, a root chakra stone. Onyx is water safe, but avoid submerging it for extended periods.

Crystals for Protection

Protective stones can be carried in your pocket or worn in jewelry (bracelets, earrings, pendants, etc.). Transform and transmute bad energy with the swirling purples of **charoite** and **amethyst**. **Tiger's eye** in gold, red, or blue helps you see through situations and clears jealousy. Use **black tourmaline**, **black obsidian**, **black onyx**, **hematite**, **jet**, or **shungite** to uproot hidden agendas and remove them. All black or metallic gray stones block negativity.

Crystals for Crystal Grids

◆

Crystal grids involve arranging gemstones, typically in a geometric pattern, on an altar or in a space to set an intention and improve overall well-being. Once all your stones are placed, create a crystalline grid of light by imagining that the stones are connected like a web. Stones that work well in a crystal grid for health include **amethyst**, **clear quartz**, **jade**, and **emerald**. When you want more harmonious interactions, turn to **angelite**, **blue lace agate**, **pink calcite**, and **selenite**. Use **watermelon tourmaline**, **kunzite**, **rhodonite**, and **rose quartz** to amplify love and kindness. Create your own luck by forming a crystal grid with **green aventurine**, **jade**, **sunstone**, and **green tourmaline**. Grids for protection can include **amethyst**, **black obsidian**, **black tourmaline**, **hematite**, **jet**, and **shungite**.

Black Tourmaline

chapter three

Black tourmaline is a great tool for grounding your spiritual practice. It and its sister stone, black tourmalinated quartz, help you center yourself and restore balance. Black tourmaline is also a good stone for empaths. Use it when you need to discern which thoughts and feelings are your own or which thoughts and feelings belong to others. This stone deflects negativity and undesirable vibes so you can feel safe and sound. Black tourmaline also deflects electromagnetic frequencies from cell phones, computers, and other electronic devices.

> **DIVINATORY MEANING:** Release the negative energetic cords of attachment that you have to past experiences and relationships. Take the wisdom from the experience but release the hurt. Step away from negative circumstances and envelop yourself in protection and blessings.

CHAKRA(S): Root

ELEMENT(S): Water

> **PAIRS WELL WITH:** Burn palo santo or cedarwood to clear your energy and the space around you. Call on the protective energy of Archangels Michael and Jehudiel to surround you with the light of protection. Essential oil clearing products are vital to restore balance and deflect anything that is not for your highest good. Heal the energetic "holes" in your auric field and restore a sense

of safety with positive affirmations like "I am safe and sound. I am out of harm's way."

NOTES: Tourmaline comes in many colors and has other benefits to offer. For example, pink, green, and watermelon tourmaline will help you connect to your heart. This stone is water safe.

Bloodstone

chapter three

Bloodstone is a stone for health and a vital life. This combination of green chalcedony and red jasper enlivens your health and encourages passionate living. Bloodstone is a perfect stone for parents to have on hand as well as adults in their childbearing years. This stone supports conscious conception and birth practices, and some people use it to support the birthing process as well. Use bloodstone to support positive vibes in any birthing process, including birthing children, art, new ideas, and so on. Bloodstone promotes the ability to recognize and acknowledge your creative ideas. Use it as motivation to bring your goals and dreams into reality.

> **DIVINATORY MEANING:** Go within using prayer, meditation, or contemplation, and align with your intentions. Self-knowledge is key. Acknowledge that your body supports you every day. Ground your spiritual practice in everyday life. Creative ideas flow through you, so be your creative self. Find balance by acknowledging and gently working through emotions and feelings.

> **CHAKRA(S):** Root, sacral

> **ELEMENT(S):** Water

> **PAIRS WELL WITH:** Use geranium essential oil to rebalance yourself. It is effective for sorting out thoughts and releasing anger and frustration. Carnelian, chrysocolla, lapis

lazuli, and sodalite are excellent matches for maintaining control and composure. *Cherry Plum*, *Holly*, and *Impatiens* Bach Flower Remedies support health and well-being by instilling patience and promoting inner peace.

NOTES: Bloodstone is most commonly dark green with red flecks. The solid dark, blood-red variety looks rich and reflects its namesake. This stone is water safe for short periods.

Crystals for Water Signs

◆

Water signs are empathic and tend to be more emotional. They are artistic, dreamy, and sometimes moody. They are sensitive: They emotionally understand another's point of view, and many water signs are empaths. Empaths can feel, know, and sometimes share another person's feelings. Here are some gemstones that amplify these signs' positive attributes.

CANCER (JUNE 22–JULY 22): The key phrase is "I feel." The Moon, a luminary, is the ruling planet of Cancer. Cancers are family-oriented, nurturing, and empathetic. **Celestite**, a pastel blue crystal, is comforting and calming, restores composure, and calms your emotions. **Moonstone** helps you trust your intuition and restores emotional balance. Keep an eye out for peach, coffee, and black moonstone. **Selenite** brings balance, grounding, and protection. Keep selenite near the entries of your home to clear energy as you go in and out.

SCORPIO (OCTOBER 24–NOVEMBER 21): The key phrase is "I desire." Scorpio, ruled by Pluto and Mars, is associated with death, taxes, inheritances, other people's money, and sex. **Black obsidian**, a form of glass created from cooling volcanic lava, helps support your passionate nature. Use it to keep negative energy at bay; it is helpful during the grieving process. **Gold tiger's eye** has a protective nature that is grounding. It supports secrecy (when appropriate), deflects jealousy, and is beneficial for stepping into your power. **Smoky quartz** supports the healing of emotional trauma. Work with smoky quartz after a cord-cutting practice to heal emotional scars.

PISCES (FEBRUARY 19–MARCH 20): The key phrase is "I believe." The watery sign of Pisces, ruled by Neptune, is associated with hidden activities, past lives, secrets, and the subconscious mind. **Amazonite**, the stone of honesty, helps you discern your truth from the truths of others. **Aquamarine** is the classic birthstone for Pisces; it helps you tap into your spiritual nature as you balance your emotions. **Larimar** is a mineral found only in the Dominican Republic, and it looks like a blue-green ocean, which supports your watery nature.

Blue Lace Agate

chapter three

Blue lace agate helps you connect with your angels. Let it be the stone for good communication with the Divine and your fellow humans too! Use blue lace agate to improve your communication skills, especially if you are shy about speaking up for yourself. This stone encourages being where you are valued and appreciated, and its pastel blue color helps you find inner peace. Gaze at blue lace agate when you are feeling uptight, and work with this gem during arguments, turmoil, or hyperactivity to restore balanced emotions.

> **DIVINATORY MEANING:** Divine timing is at play in your life. You are always in the right place at the right time. Opportunities are all around you. Recognize them and act upon them with peaceful energy. Release aggressive vibes and communicate calmly.
>
> **CHAKRA(S):** Throat
>
> **ELEMENT(S):** Air, water
>
> **PAIRS WELL WITH:** Crystals with a vibrational match are angelite, aquamarine, blue calcite, and kyanite. Use an aromatherapeutic essential oil mist to improve communication and align with the truth; tea tree essential oil is ideal for actualizing a connection with angelic communication and guidance. Several animal allies resonate

with the vibration of blue lace agate, including Bat, Blue Jay, Dolphin, and Parrot.

NOTES: This pastel blue agate without the "lace"—the white patterns—is known as blue chalcedony. This stone is water safe, but avoid extended periods of submersion.

Carnelian

chapter three

Carnelian promotes creativity and action. Use it when writing your to-do list, then keep it nearby to tackle each chore or goal easily. This stone helps you find the courage to start and finish creative projects, so use it to manifest your desired reality. Keep a piece of carnelian in your peripheral vision to remind you to maintain momentum when writing or working on any inspirational project. Carnelian helps you embrace emotions and challenges, accept them, and move on. It's a perfect companion when releasing emotional blocks. Carnelian is a stone of fertility in body, mind, and spirit.

> **DIVINATORY MEANING:** Envision your future with joy and hope. You are fertile with good ideas. Allow yourself the time to create. Courageously bring your ideas into actuality. You have the vision and wherewithal to conceive something magnificent. Self-acceptance and self-knowledge provide the foundation for attaining great heights. Pay attention to the visions, ideas, and innovative approaches in your daily life and creative projects.
>
> **CHAKRA(S):** Sacral
>
> **ELEMENT(S):** Fire
>
> **PAIRS WELL WITH:** Match carnelian with this positive affirmation to amplify its effect: "I am creative and bring my ideas into reality. Creativity flows through me in many

facets of my life." Peacock copper, garnet, and ruby are gems to increase passion on all levels of awareness. Inhale the sweet and sunny scent of orange essential oil to bring spiritual fortitude and self-confidence. *Larch*, a Bach Flower Remedy, amplifies courage and improves your ability to integrate life.

NOTES: Carnelian is the orange-red variety of chalcedony. You can often find it in a solid deep orange, but there are also banded varieties as well as carnelian with druzy inclusions. This stone is water safe.

Crystals for Careers in the Pursuit of Knowledge

Phantom quartz is a good ally for intuitives and psychics because it encourages you to trust gut feelings and decipher intuitive hunches. **Zebra jasper** reminds you to look and think clearly, necessary qualities for journalists. It helps you see what is plain as day as well as what is written between the lines. **Clear quartz** helps with objective observation, which is required of scientists. Use clear quartz to align with evidence and process it systematically.

Crystals to Connect with Animal Allies

The characteristics of animals—from birds and insects to mammals, fish, and reptiles—relate to our human journey on this planet, providing us with lessons and helping us mindfully focus our intentions. Match the qualities of gemstones to the teachings of animal allies for a deeper understanding of yourself and life in general. Here are a few allies and their vibrationally matching gems: Bear teaches the value of grounded awareness and listening; pair with **brown agate**, **brown jasper**, and **honey calcite**. Blue Jay helps you find your voice as well as the courage to set boundaries using gems like **amazonite**, **angelite**, **aquamarine**, **blue calcite**, **blue lace agate**, **celestite**, and **citrine**. Stones like **amethyst**, **charoite**, **pietersite**, and **tiger's eye** are transformational stones that pair with Butterfly energy. Butterfly helps you realize that even the smallest of changes in your perception or the way you think can change your life significantly. With Cardinal as your ally, amplify your personal power and ability to shine your magnificence with **garnet**, **red goldstone**, **ruby**, and **vanadinite** supporting you.

Charoite

chapter three

The swirling energy of charoite activates the crown chakra for psychic development and spiritual awakening. Use this as your ally when you are going through spiritual transformation. Charoite is a stone of metamorphosis. Use it to untangle chaotic thoughts, and wear it or keep it nearby during challenges and periods of change. Partner with the stone when you feel vulnerable and shore up your ability to control your life. This is a great crystal to use when you need courage. Employ this gem to increase your confidence and ability to set boundaries; it supports time alone for thinking and contemplating. Hold a piece of charoite when you pause for introspection and reflection.

> DIVINATORY MEANING: Take notice of the energy you pick up from others. Then, go within and release the chaos. You have the strength you need. Shed light on confusing circumstances as you ground yourself in your spiritual practice. Restore your inner strength and amplify your personal power.
>
> CHAKRA(S): Crown, third eye, solar plexus
>
> ELEMENT(S): Water
>
> PAIRS WELL WITH: Connect with Beetle, an ally who can help you be flexible as you work through challenging situations while maintaining strong external protection.

Charoite assists in the process of spiritual transformation, and beetles go through a complete metamorphosis, which is a keyword for charoite. Call on Archangel Zadkiel to transmute unwanted energy and cultivate the freedom to be all you can be.

NOTES: Charoite has many minerals swirling within. It is found in shades of purple, often with yellow or black inclusions. This stone is water safe if quickly rinsed and dried—do not immerse charoite in water.

Citrine

chapter three

Citrine is the yellow variety of quartz. Use this stone to amplify happiness, joy, and confidence. Let the radiant vibes of citrine support your ability to set boundaries with others and speak up for yourself when necessary. Citrine helps with feelings of overwhelm; use it to digest life as well as food! The golden rays of this stone can help improve digestive challenges. Throughout the ages, citrine has been known as the "merchant's stone" because it increases abundance. Keep a piece in your purse, wallet, or wherever you keep your money. Invite and accept abundance, wealth, and good fortune with this stone in hand.

DIVINATORY MEANING: Shine your light and allow others to see your magnificence. It is safe to be powerful. Focus on what you do well and increase your self-esteem. Prosperity is yours! Whatever you desire, imagine, and passionately act upon will become a reality. You can reach your full potential.

CHAKRA(S): Solar plexus

ELEMENT(S): Fire

PAIRS WELL WITH: Citrus essential oils (such as bergamot, grapefruit, lemon, lime, and orange) support you in creating a happy and productive life. Citrus oils are phototoxic; therefore, avoid exposure to direct sunlight when using topically. Spray an aromatherapeutic mist to amplify joy, personal power, self-confidence, mental clarity, and the ability to shine your light. Incorporate some or all of these Bach Flower Remedies to amplify the positive qualities of citrine: *Aspen*, *Cerato*, *Gentian*, *Larch*, *Willow*, and *Vervain*.

NOTES: This yellow quartz is found in tumbled form, clusters, points, and cathedrals. The burnt orange variety of citrine is usually heat-treated amethyst—natural citrine ranges from a clear light yellow to a smoky brown yellow. This stone is water safe.

Creating a Gemstone Essence for Energetic Mists

◆

To make a gemstone essence, set an intention. Then place the corresponding stone(s) in a glass jar with a lid while focusing on why you are creating this essence. Cover the stone(s) with water as you fill the jar about three-quarters of the way. Add approximately one tablespoon of grain alcohol (151 proof, or your choice of high-proof liquor) to stabilize the vibrational essence. Close the lid on the jar tightly, then wipe the jar with a towel to dry off any moisture. Create a label and adhere to the jar. Allow the gemstone essence to sit undisturbed for about twenty-four hours. Then, add one or two tablespoons of the energetic mix to a two-ounce spray bottle. Fill the rest of the spray bottle with water or an essential oil blend. Spray the mist around you and your space while keeping the intention of the blend in mind. You can leave the crystal in the jar indefinitely, using the gemstone essence to refresh your mist as needed.

Crystals for a Charm Bag

Set an intention, then gather three or four different crystals that align with your intention and place them in a charm bag. You can carry the charm bag around your neck, in your pocket, or in your purse, or you can put the charm bag near your bedside or the place where you spend most of your time. Use **green aventurine**, **jade**, and **emerald** for health and overall well-being. **Blue chalcedony**, **sodalite**, and **chrysoprase** are perfect for a charm bag for peace. Place **rose quartz**, **pink calcite**, and **ruby in zoisite** in a charm bag for love and kindness. If you need protection, **black tourmaline**, **hematite**, and **shungite** will deflect negative vibes.

Chrysocolla

chapter three

Chrysocolla is a mix of malachite, azurite, cuprite, other copper minerals, and rock crystal quartz. This stone is blue, green, and brown and looks much like the earth; its energy can help you remember that you are a steward of the earth. Chrysocolla can help you achieve balance; its blue-green energy is like a healing salve. It is an excellent choice for reducing inflamed energies, whether there is an inflamed state of consciousness or inflammation in the body. This copper-based mineral is good for calming anger in cooperation with the foundational azurite-malachite composition of chrysocolla, so use chrysocolla for meditative and contemplative work when you need extra help to calm your mind and soothe aggravation.

> **DIVINATORY MEANING:** Open your heart center and allow healing. Find your voice and express your thoughts and prayers to restore balance. Take action to reclaim your inner peace by exercising and practicing healthy communication. Nurture yourself.
>
> **CHAKRA(S):** All
>
> **ELEMENT(S):** Earth
>
> **PAIRS WELL WITH:** Call on Archangel Raphael with chrysocolla in hand to align with healing support for discomfort on all levels: mentally, emotionally, physically, and spiritually. The *Vine* Bach Flower Remedy

can calm aggressiveness. The earthy aroma of spikenard embodies inner peace and nurturance, and its calming vibration slows inner chatter and helps you sort things out. Use spikenard with chrysocolla to reduce agitation and irritability, or blend spikenard with lavender to balance your emotions.

NOTES: This stone is water safe. Avoid submersion for extended periods.

Chrysoprase

chapter three

Chrysoprase encourages nurturing practices. It helps you expand your awareness and focus on allowing loving and kind experiences in your life. Use chrysoprase to open yourself to unlimited potential. This beautiful green stone is soothing and healing. When you rest, leave chrysoprase near the thymus to realign the heart chakra. Turn to this gem for help when you feel overwhelmed, as it can improve self-confidence and personal power. Chrysoprase can be supportive if you have the blues and want to lift yourself out of depression.

>   **DIVINATORY MEANING:** Open your ears, mind, and heart to connect with the cosmos, and invite higher spiritual communication. Relax! Allow your compassionate side to come to the forefront. Healthy nourishment is a priority.
>
>   **CHAKRA(S):** Heart, throat
>
>   **ELEMENT(S):** Water
>
>   **PAIRS WELL WITH:** Call on the assistance of Saint Hildegard of Bingen to heal past injustices or memories of abuse. Allow her vibration to feel nurturing and empowering. Work with *Oak* Bach Flower Remedy to help you recover after periods of struggle. Inhale lemon essential oil to restore your confidence. Lemon, when used in conjunction with chrysoprase, will help you refresh yourself on

all levels. Combine chrysoprase with rose quartz, pink calcite, and other pink-colored gemstones to feel loved and loving, or pair it with emerald and jade for optimism and hope. State affirmations like "I am nurtured and nurturing. Love fills my body, mind, and soul."

NOTES: Chrysoprase has a beautiful seafoam green color that is healing to gaze at, though this variety of chalcedony can be found in various shades of green. This stone is water safe. Avoid prolonged exposure to direct sunlight to prevent color fading.

Crystals for Manifestation and Success

♦

Crystals are tools for manifesting and creating success. Put your intention into a stone by gazing at it and acknowledging that every time you touch it, look at it, or think of it, it will help you refocus your attention and awareness on your intention, bringing you closer to the reality being created. The use of crystals goes beyond wearing a stone as a piece of jewelry or carrying a stone around in your pocket, purse, or briefcase; start incorporating gemstones into your daily life. You can even place gemstones in your pillowcase at night: First, focus on your desired intention, then allow them to work while you sleep.

Clearing and Charging Your Crystals

There are many methods for clearing and charging crystals: Clear your stones with various herbs and resins. Clear your crystals with water if the stone is water safe. (Most stones that end in -ite are not water safe.) You can take crystals to the beach and rinse them in the ocean, but I've lost a few crystals this way. A very simple, low-cost method is to run tap water over your crystals to clear them. If you use water to clear your crystals, don't leave them in water for long—just rinse the gem and dry it immediately. Many polished stones lose their shine or finish after being submerged in water, or they become mottled if they aren't dried quickly. You can use telepathy to clear and charge crystals and other objects. You might also enjoy the ritual of placing your stones outside in the moonlight or sunlight to charge.

Clear Quartz

chapter three

Clear quartz corresponds with every color because of its full light spectrum. It can be charged easily: Hold a piece of clear quartz in your hand, think good thoughts, and visualize positive outcomes. Then, use that stone to transmit and transduce energy. With clear quartz in hand, send out vibrations of goodness, love, and well-being. Visualize your desired outcome or personal reality. Amplify the intention that things will work out for the highest good. When directed, clear quartz will amplify other gemstones' qualities as well as your thoughts. Clear quartz can help you stay focused, so it's especially beneficial to hold or gaze at during meditation and contemplation.

> DIVINATORY MEANING: You are an amazing being of light with wisdom and knowledge. Acknowledge this and take your own sage advice. You have clarity, so allow yourself to see the bigger picture. If you look at things from a higher perspective, you'll gain understanding.
>
> CHAKRA(S): All
>
> ELEMENT(S): All
>
> PAIRS WELL WITH: Inhale the floral, fresh fragrance of lavender essential oil during meditation while holding clear quartz in your hand. This is a nice combination that brings grounding and peace. Let the calming vibrations of lavender and clear quartz comfort you

and calm chaotic situations. Share good thoughts such as "I feel serene. I am relaxed. I am healthy, whole, and complete."

NOTES: Clear quartz is the transparent variety of quartz. The other members of the quartz family include amethyst, citrine, rose quartz, and smoky quartz. This stone is water safe.

Fluorite

chapter three

Fluorite is known as the "genius stone." Use it to improve your innate intelligence and sense of focus. It is ideal for meditation and contemplation because it helps clear the mind of extraneous thoughts. Fluorite's natural configuration has a resemblance to the motherboard in a computer, and it supports logical thinking and brainpower. Fluorite is found in a variety of colors, and you can work with the colors of the stone to fine-tune and calibrate the energy of the corresponding chakra. Fluorite is grounding yet elevates your consciousness, bringing higher awareness to ordinary reality.

DIVINATORY MEANING: Quiet your mind. Brighten up. Remember you are intelligent. Develop and cultivate your inner genius. Uncover new information to develop your ideas, and complete tasks with ease. You can accomplish whatever you focus on. Organization is key!

CHAKRA(S): Crown, third eye, throat, heart, solar plexus

ELEMENT(S): Water

PAIRS WELL WITH: Sandalwood essential oil or fragrance activates the wise scholar within. It can also be used to clear thoughts during meditation. Lemon and lime essential oils bring mental clarity and alertness, raise awareness, and increase joy. Place a drop of one of these essential oils in a diffuser or on a hanky for mental and emotional clarity. To remember your innate intelligence, say, "I am smart enough. I can focus on and complete complex tasks."

NOTES: Fluorite comes in a rainbow of colors, though it is most commonly green, purple, clear, yellow, or teal blue. This stone is water safe. Avoid submersion for extended periods. Avoid salt water.

Crystals for Grief and Mourning

Grief and mourning are deeply profound and personal. Keeping a few gems nearby or in jewelry can support you through the process. Whether grieving a loved one or a way of life, let these sparkling treasures help you find hope and light within. **Apache tears** are black obsidian, which naturally forms during the cooling of volcanic lava. Apache tears help cope with the grief associated with suicide; this stone's name stems from a legend about Apache warriors who ended a conflict by choosing suicide over surrender. **Chrysoprase**, a heart chakra stone, heightens compassion for oneself. This seafoam-green stone encourages nurturing practices. **Rhodonite**, a stone for restoration, is helpful to find balance after losing a loved one. Rhodonite can help restore your emotional body; use it to remind yourself to take time to recover and relax. **Rose quartz** is the ultimate stone of loving-kindness, so it is perfect for self-love. This rosy gem aligns your consciousness with divine love, compassion, mercy, tolerance, and kindness.

Crystals for Careers in Healing

Green tourmaline supports doctors and nurses. It activates healing, compassion, mercy, kindness, and love. First responders benefit from **sodalite** as it brings calmness, which is necessary in emergencies. Use it to deal with turmoil, disasters, fear, anger, and frustration. **Apophyllite** is a stone of universal wisdom, which makes it the perfect stone for holistic healers. Use it to improve meditation and inner work.

Garnet

chapter three

Garnet awakens the sleeping force that holds your full potential within you. Work with this stone to activate your creative power. It is also a great stone to use for manifestation, as it prevents procrastination and awakens motivation. Visualize your intentions when partnering with garnet. This stone can be used for self-empowerment. Garnet benefits heart-centered focus and communication, so emanate loving vibes with this stone in hand. Use garnet as a reminder to honor your boundaries and ethics. You can even gaze at red garnet when you feel tired to wake yourself up and ground yourself.

> DIVINATORY MEANING: There is plenty of energy and joy. Be willing to share your passion. Strength is yours. Take charge of a situation—stay determined and forge ahead to complete your goals or tasks. Use your vitality to live a full and abundant life. You are healthy at the core of your being. Open your heart. Allow love.

CHAKRA(S): Root, sacral, heart

ELEMENT(S): Fire

PAIRS WELL WITH: Place a drop of *Hornbeam* Bach Flower Remedy in your water to overcome procrastination. Working with garnet and *Hornbeam* Bach Flower Remedy on a daily basis will help you stay motivated and complete tasks. Shift your mindset by sharing positive thoughts like "It is easy for me to take action and move forward. I have the interest and strength to bring my ideas into reality."

NOTES: Garnet comes in a variety of colors, most commonly red. Keep an eye out for green garnet, known as grossularite. Orange-brown garnet is hessonite, and reddish-purple garnet is called rhodolite. This stone is water safe for a minute or two. Avoid submersion.

Green Aventurine

chapter three

Green aventurine is the good luck stone of the gemstone kingdom. Use it to attract abundance, healthy relationships, happiness, and all that is good. This is the ideal crystal for attracting a happy, loving partner. Because this green gem is a stone of prosperity, you can partner it with citrine to attract extreme wealth. Green aventurine also helps attract and maintain a balanced, healthy view of life. It's a stone of health, so use it to calm anger and stress and to heal your heart on all levels: mentally, physically, emotionally, and spiritually. This gem is an ally when focusing on a gratitude practice; hold on to a piece of green aventurine as you express gratitude for all the blessings in your life.

> **DIVINATORY MEANING:** You are incredibly lucky, and you create your own luck and good fortune. You will have plenty of money and plenty to share. If you focus on your vast abundance, you will attract even more of it. Savor your friendships and connections with others.
>
> **CHAKRA(S):** Heart
>
> **ELEMENT(S):** Earth, water
>
> **PAIRS WELL WITH:** When it comes to luck, it is always up to you and your mindset to attract favorable circumstances. Share positive statements like "My imagination is the key to my success. I am so incredibly lucky."

Combine affirmations with other lucky gems, like clear quartz and jade, and an aromatherapeutic mist to activate good fortune and blessings in your life.

NOTES: Green aventurine is available in various depths of color. Aventurine is available in colors other than green. This stone is water safe. Avoid soaking for extended periods.

Crystals for Good Communication

Communication develops strong relationships. Peaceful communication is helpful for healthy exchanges, so include **blue lace agate** to improve harmonious vibes and become conscious of communication components—sharing and listening are both vital factors. **Larimar** and **tabular quartz** help improve telepathic communication: heart-to-heart and mind-to-mind expression. Knowing your personal truth is another factor in healthy exchanges; **amazonite** and **turquoise** are helpful when you know the truth and want to communicate with integrity. Elevate your spiritual experiences with **angelite** and **celestite** to listen to guidance from spirit guides, angels, and loved ones on the other side.

Crystals for Cultivating Relationships

◆

Clusters create an atmosphere of community coming together and working in harmony; use **amethyst**, **celestite**, **citrine**, and **clear quartz** to create a good atmosphere for your family and friends. **Dalmatian jasper** promotes loyal and honest friends and colleagues. **Amazonite**, the stone of truth, encourages honesty and integrity in yourself and your colleagues. For romance, **garnet** awakens the desire to be in a romantic relationship and increases the need for romance and seduction. Use it to remain open to doing whatever it takes to make a relationship work. **Kunzite** amplifies the vibration of love and magnetizes the love of your life. **Rose quartz** increases kindness and thoughtfulness. **Ruby in fuchsite** and **ruby in zoisite** open your heart and ignite passion in your relationship.

Green Moss Agate

chapter three

Hold a piece of green moss agate to the light to gain perspective and a view of the natural world encapsulated in a crystal. This agate has a heart-centered, grounding influence that aligns you with nature. Use it as an ally when you work with aromatherapy or herbs. Let green moss agate remind you of your role as an earth steward. This crystal is a portal into the world of fairies, gnomes, and elves. Recognize your intimate connection with Mother Earth and the world of holistic health.

>**DIVINATORY MEANING:** Release emotional ties from the past. Imagine toxic thoughts and emotions transforming into rich fertilizer for future life experiences. Spend time in nature and feel the power of the planet's green energy. Recognize the interconnectedness of trees, plants, animals, and all life. Behave as if the Divine in all life matters.
>
>**CHAKRA(S):** Heart, root
>
>**ELEMENT(S):** Earth
>
>**PAIRS WELL WITH:** Cedar trees have the vibration of Earth Keeper, a steward of this planet. Work with cedar in various forms (including essential oils, leaves, or incense) to reclaim your balance through nature. Allow green moss agate to encourage you to spend time outdoors.

Go hug a tree! Complementary stones are citrine, petrified wood, and tree agate. Invite and invoke Archangel Thuriel and Saint Francis of Assisi to amplify the benefits of this stone.

NOTES: Green moss agate ranges from translucent to opaque. It has green, fernlike sprays within clear quartz—hold a piece to the light to see the little forest within. This stone is water safe, but do not submerge it in water.

Hematite

chapter three

Hematite is an earthy, grounding force. Use this stone to deflect negativity and maintain focus when you feel scattered. This is the stone for you if you are easily distracted! Grab a piece or wear a hematite bracelet to focus your energy and ground yourself. Hold a piece of hematite and feel your connection to the earth through the soles of your feet. Hematite is known to calm and stabilize chaotic vibes, so use it when you are taking on the feelings and energies of others and need to shift your awareness to maintain a sacred space.

> **DIVINATORY MEANING:** Quiet your thoughts. Become aware of what's circling around in your mind. It is time to transform a negative situation. Transform that energy into focused peace and deep rest. Calm any excess energy and center yourself for positive results.
>
> **CHAKRA(S):** Root
>
> **ELEMENT(S):** Earth
>
> **PAIRS WELL WITH:** Porcupine is a good ally when you feel vulnerable or challenged by the energy of others. Call on Porcupine's vibe to help you discern between being mindful of who you are around and sharing what is on your mind. Amber, in its many forms, can help maintain sacred space. An amber bracelet or the scent

of amber will lend you the courage to set boundaries with grace.

NOTES: This shiny, metallic, black-to-steel-gray stone sometimes has a sparkly appearance, known as specular hematite. This stone is not water safe.

Crystals and Essential Oils for Motivation, Creativity, and Prosperity

◆

Cinnamon and **sunstone** support passionate action to achieve your goals and dreams. They work together to boost confidence and the courage to fulfill your unlimited potential. Use this combo to earn unlimited income doing what you love. Cinnamon helps you tap into your creativity and brings ideas to the forefront. The brilliant energy of sunstone increases the personal power needed to succeed. Financial success is yours, but action is required. Bring your ideas into actuality. Radiate self-confidence. Act with faith. Manifest to create your reality. Enjoy life and embrace passionate living! *Cinnamon may inhibit blood clotting, so avoid use if on anticoagulants. Do not use if pregnant or nursing.*

Crystals and Essential Oils for Intuition and Spiritual Connection

Frankincense and **apophyllite** are allies that can improve communication, spiritual awareness, mindfulness, and psychic abilities. Frankincense is the ultimate essential oil to align with higher consciousness. Combined with apophyllite, it brings clarity and connects you to universal wisdom and the Akashic records. Apophyllite supports the intention to clear your mind of incessant chatter, bringing clear knowing. Inhale the scent of frankincense to maximize your intuitive skills. Open your consciousness and listen for your soul's truth.

Jade

chapter three

Jade is the stone of good fortune. Use this gem to amplify gratitude and focus on existing blessings. Jade can be used to improve your manifesting skills; experience jade's vibe to magically manifest extraordinary wealth and abundance on all levels. Visualization with jade in hand brings beneficial results. Think loving thoughts and work with jade to increase your belief that you have extraordinarily good luck. With jade as a reminder, take the time to be grateful for every little thing. Use jade to balance and align your health, vital energy, and finances so you have plenty of money to cover your core needs of food, water, and shelter.

> DIVINATORY MEANING: You will attract money, joy, happiness, and good fortune. You are a blessing, and you are blessed. Believe in good fortune and it will be yours. You live a charmed life.
>
> CHAKRA(S): Heart, solar plexus
>
> ELEMENT(S): Air
>
> PAIRS WELL WITH: Incorporate green aventurine and citrine to increase wealth, luck, and abundance. Call on Archangel Uriel to illuminate your awareness and spark your personal power to experience extraordinary wealth and altruism. Say, "I am inspired with practical

solutions to challenges and with ideas that bring goodness and prosperity to all people."

NOTES: Jade is most commonly found in its green form, but be on the lookout for jade in shades of white, gray, black, yellow, orange, or purple-violet. This stone is water safe under running water; do not submerge in water.

Lapis Lazuli

chapter three

Lapis lazuli contains calcite, sodalite, and pyrite. This crystal's deep blue color is calming. Lapis lazuli is beneficial when you are dealing with emotional turmoil. Use it to release agitation, anger, and frustration and to calm inflammation. It's great for meditation and helps improve focus and concentration. Use it to awaken your intuitive senses and invoke help from archangels, especially Archangel Michael. Tap into the Akashic records with this stone as a guiding force. Lapis lazuli is also beneficial for dream recall and interpretation.

> DIVINATORY MEANING: Listen to your voice within. Trust your intuition. Follow your internal guidance and believe in your hunches. Breathe deeply. Calm yourself and find peace. Tap into the entourage of angels available to help you every day.
>
> CHAKRA(S): Crown, third eye
>
> ELEMENT(S): Fire
>
> PAIRS WELL WITH: Sodalite, one of the components of lapis lazuli, is a great grounding tool when channeling and using your psychic abilities. Amplify the effects of lapis lazuli with aromatherapeutic mists that promote connection with the Akashic and the Divine. Lapis lazuli is a good companion for emergence caregivers who

work as birth and death guides to support the beginning and end of life on this planet.

NOTES: Lapis lazuli is a dark blue stone with metallic gold flecks. This stone is not water safe. It can be cleaned with a cloth and water as long as it is quickly dried, but do not submerge lapis lazuli.

Crystals for Intuition: Clairgustation

◆

Clairgustation is the ability to taste something that isn't in the mouth. This inherent psychic sense could signal a visit or message from loved ones on the other side. The olfactory nerve, taste buds, and cranial nerves become sensitive to the presence of the spirit or a message from the Divine that gets delivered through the sense of taste. **Apatite, peridot, prehnite**, and **serpentine** are stones associated with digestion and pair well with improving your psychic sense of taste. The golden vibrations of **citrine** and **golden calcite** support the confidence to employ this tool.

Crystals for Oracle and Tarot Card Readers

When reading for others, gemstones are allies that encourage you to trust your intuition and help you find the words to express yourself. **Clear quartz** helps you tap into divine inspiration and brings clarity. A handheld clear quartz point about four to six inches in length is helpful when tuning in to a client or doing a session for yourself. Other quartz crystals like **elestial quartz, smoky quartz, Herkimer diamond**, and **record keeper quartz** can help you tap into the knowledge and wisdom needed in a card reading. **Black tourmaline** points or logs create a protecting and grounding vibration. **Selenite** and **kyanite** provide balance and align you and a client. **Amber** is good for establishing a healthy boundary between you and a client.

Magenta-Dyed Agate

chapter three

This brilliant pink stone encourages passion, joy, and fortitude. Use magenta-dyed agate as a reminder to practice self-care, balance your emotions, and improve confidence within your relationships. Use this color-enhanced stone to enrich your relationships of all kinds, as magenta-dyed agate supports love, loyalty, and emotional security. Use it to increase and experience compassion, kindness, and wisdom. Magenta-dyed agate is an ally for those with children and assists in their responsibility to be a good parent.

> **DIVINATORY MEANING:** Open your heart. Allow love—radiate love. Establish healthy boundaries to care for yourself and those you love. Hold a vision and imagine a better way of life for all beings. Permit yourself to embrace rest, and nurture your creative ideas.
>
> **CHAKRA(S):** Heart
>
> **ELEMENT(S):** Air
>
> **PAIRS WELL WITH:** This magenta stone is aligned with the vibration of Saint Mary Magdalene, the feminine Christ. Work with Mary Magdalene's energy to amplify unconditional love. Use frankincense, spikenard, or sweet marjoram essential oil to amplify self-care and balance for inner peace and calm. Add other crystals like cobaltoan calcite, kunzite, pink calcite, pink opal,

rhodonite, rhodochrosite, and rose quartz to find love in all of life's situations. Magenta-dyed agate pairs well with Penguin, an animal ally for joining with a loyal and dedicated mate.

NOTES: Because magenta-dyed agate is man-made, this stone is not water safe. The dye will leak out if this stone comes in contact with water and could stain the surface it is on.

Moldavite

chapter three

Moldavite is the stone of a visionary. Use this stone to have the courage and confidence to create a business or source of income that you love. Moldavite opens a flow of information, ideas, and actions. Working with this crystal can transform your life! Because moldavite is a naturally formed glass associated with meteoric activity, it is the perfect gem for allowing far-out concepts into your consciousness. Envision the whole process to completion so that it can be easily adapted into reality.

DIVINATORY MEANING: Use your brilliant mind to look at life from a higher perspective. Be a channel for otherworldly concepts. Recall processes and knowledge from prior incarnations. Heart-centered action combined with grounded inspiration will bring success and financial gain. Focus on love, peace, and harmony.

CHAKRA(S): Crown, heart, root

ELEMENT(S): Water, fire

PAIRS WELL WITH: Use pyrite to ground your out-of-this-world experience with moldavite. Call on Archangel Metatron (previously known as Enoch) to activate higher states of consciousness, tap into the Akashic records, and awaken your awareness of your soul's evolution. Invite the Angel of Creative Intelligence to inspire financial success. The high vibrations of bergamot and grapefruit essential oils will automatically raise your consciousness and awareness to receive messages. However, citrus oils are phototoxic, so avoid exposure to direct sunlight if using them topically. With moldavite nearby, affirm, "I am conscious and awake. I believe in unlimited possibilities."

NOTES: This emerald-to-olive-green glass is sometimes found on the market as man-made moldavite. Natural moldavite will have bubbles or inclusions. This stone is water safe.

Crystals for Journeying

Journeying is an opportunity to go deep within your consciousness to gain insight, understanding, ideas, realizations, and healing. Drumming can be used to guide the process, as it brings you to a trancelike state to deepen the experience. Crystals can also aid in your journeying. **Black obsidian, black tourmaline, smoky quartz,** and **tourmalinated quartz** are grounding and protective stones. Use **cobra jasper, leopardskin jasper,** and **zebra jasper** to encourage flexibility and a deeper understanding of the experience. **Golden calcite** and **orange calcite** increase courage and improve confidence and adaptability. Connect with the lessons from past lives using **petrified wood**. Finally, gain clarity and tap into your intuition and the Akashic records with **chrysocolla, clear quartz, elestial quartz,** and **Herkimer diamond**.

Crystals for Caregivers

I spent many years caring for my parents in their elder years, which was extremely rewarding. I'd never trade the experience, though it was exhausting and debilitating. Self-care for the caregiver is of utmost importance. **Chrysoprase**, a beautiful seafoam-green stone, increases feelings of self-love. Its nurturing vibration reminds you how important it is to take care of yourself too. Be sure to bring the stone in direct contact with your skin. **Black tourmaline** will keep your space clear and free of unwanted vibes. Use **kunzite** to radiate love in a wide circumference all around you. Finally, consider getting a fist-size tumbled **rose quartz** that can be placed on your heart center to realign and energize.

Moonstone

chapter three

Moonstone helps you trust your intuitive hunches. This stone of receptivity is the gem for improving intuition and psychic senses. Moonstone is good for inner reflection and meditation; gaze at the adularescent moonstone shimmer as you quiet your mind. You can use moonstone to connect with the Goddess or Divine Feminine. Moonstone is also a great stone for restful sleep and pleasant dreams. Put a small piece in your pillowcase or on your nightstand for better dream recall and interpretation.

> **DIVINATORY MEANING:** You have extraordinary awareness; align with the moon's cycles for higher awareness. Self-knowledge brings mental clarity. Pay attention to your dreams and interpret their symbolic meaning. You are intuitive—believe in yourself when you feel or know something about a situation that isn't obvious to others.

> **CHAKRA(S):** Crown, third eye, solar plexus, sacral

> **ELEMENT(S):** Water

> **PAIRS WELL WITH:** Labradorite helps you reflect on your inner knowing. While labradorite is not technically a moonstone, some varieties are called moonstone, so this is the perfect combination. Jasmine and neroli essential oils support moonstone's receptive nature and increase nurturing vibrations. *Clematis* Bach Flower Remedy helps

you remain mindful and present in any given moment, which allows for higher receptivity of intuitive messages.

NOTES: Moonstone is found in many colors: milky white; transparent, reflective white; beige or brown; gray; peach; black; and rainbow, which has shimmery adularescence and, at times, blue flash. This stone is water safe.

Orange Calcite

chapter three

Orange calcite invites an optimistic outlook, so use it to increase joy and happiness. Orange calcite is an ally when working out or doing physical training, as it supports muscle and bone strength. You can even use orange calcite for positive effects on the alignment of the spine. Orange calcite is the perfect stone to work with when going through changes; keep it nearby to increase courage, confidence, and self-worth. It can bring strength when you have to set boundaries with others. Orange calcite is also great for fertility and creativity.

> **DIVINATORY MEANING:** Change is inevitable. Embrace change and recognize that you create your life experiences. Trust the process of change while honoring your feelings. You are blessed with creative ideas—dare to bring them into reality.
>
> **CHAKRA(S):** Solar plexus, sacral
>
> **ELEMENT(S):** Water
>
> **PAIRS WELL WITH:** The animal ally Crocodile supports you when you need to let go of old ways of doing things. With the help of Crocodile and orange calcite, embrace adaptability and patience. Mandarin essential oil is beneficial for increasing confidence and shifting from a negative outlook to a positive one. However, citrus oils are phototoxic, so avoid exposure to direct sunlight when

using them topically. During times of change, *Walnut* Bach Flower Remedy supports transitioning from one way of being to another.

NOTES: Orange calcite can be found in a creamy orange or yellow color. This stone is not water safe. However, orange calcite can be rinsed for cleansing purposes as long as it is dried immediately.

Crystals and Essential Oils for Happiness and Self-Confidence

Grapefruit and **citrine** partner to strengthen your self-esteem and the courage to shine your light brightly. Grapefruit essential oil expands your awareness of blessings, joy, and happiness. Citrine does the same and rids your consciousness of doubt and fear. Use this pair to bring more joy into your life. *Grapefruit oil is phototoxic; therefore, avoid exposure to direct sunlight when using topically.*

Crystals for the Chakras

◆

The human body has seven primary chakras that regulate us on all levels: mentally, emotionally, physically, and spiritually. Each chakra has a color associated with it, and the colors of gemstones can correspond with the colors of the chakras. The seventh chakra (also known as the crown chakra) is violet and white, and **amethyst, apophyllite, clear quartz,** and **selenite** are corresponding stones. The third eye chakra's color is indigo, and some sixth chakra stones are **blue sapphire, charoite, lapis lazuli, sodalite,** and **sugilite**. The throat chakra is pastel blue to turquoise in color, and **amazonite, angelite, aquamarine, celestite,** and **turquoise** gems correlate with the fifth chakra. The fourth chakra (heart chakra) is like a bridge between the upper three chakras (spiritual) and the lower three (physical). Use pink and green stones at this center, such as **green aventurine, green jade, green tourmaline, emerald, kunzite, rubellite (pink tourmaline), rose quartz,** and **watermelon tourmaline** to name just a few. Yellow is associated with the third chakra (solar plexus chakra); **citrine, golden calcite, golden topaz, tiger's eye,** and **yellow fluorite** are perfect pairings. The second chakra (sacral chakra) is orange, so it pairs well with orange stones like **carnelian, orange calcite, red goldstone,** and **red jasper**. The first chakra (root chakra) is red, but it also has brown, black, and metallic vibes, so use **black tourmaline, garnet, hematite, pyrite, ruby,** and **smoky quartz**.

Peridot

chapter three

Peridot, also known as olivine, is a stone of healing and transformation. It's a powerful crystal for rising above challenges, including addiction. Wear a piece of peridot or keep one in your pocket while going through a rite of passage. Peridot is ideal for the wounded healer, those who have had painful experiences being empathetic and compassionate. Empaths benefit from the vibes of this green stone because it supports personal power through awareness. Reiki practitioners would benefit from having peridot nearby during a healing session. Use peridot to transmute self-sabotage and agitation. This gem is especially helpful for dissolving jealousy—either the jealousy you are feeling or the jealousy others direct at you.

DIVINATORY MEANING: Recognize your good fortune, then feel authentic happiness for the good fortune of others. Be discerning about who you let into your personal space.

CHAKRA(S): Heart, solar plexus

ELEMENT(S): Fire

PAIRS WELL WITH: *Willow* Bach Flower Remedy is helpful when you are feeling jealous or angry because of others' successes. When combined with peridot, tiger's eye (in blue, gold, or red) helps deflect jealousy from others; rosemary essential oil also deflects jealous vibes. Invoke Archangel Sabrael to release jealousy of any kind. Amethyst pairs well with peridot for transforming and transmuting challenges. From an astrological perspective, peridot is helpful when working with Chiron in your natal chart.

NOTES: Peridot, pronounced PAIR-uh-doh, ranges from olive green to chartreuse. This stone is water safe if you are rinsing it as part of your cleansing process. Avoid prolonged exposure to water.

Purple-Dyed Agate

chapter three

The transformational power of this stone awakens your spiritual sight and helps you discern the truth about people and situations. Purple-dyed agate helps clear jealousy, negative self-talk, confusion, and chaos. Use purple-dyed agate to learn what needs to dissolve from your life for your highest good and to amplify an aura of peace and protection. Purple-dyed agate is especially powerful when you need to lovingly release people from your life.

> **DIVINATORY MEANING:** Make changes in your life to manifest health and well-being. Choose peaceful people and places to support you in living your best life. Discernment is important—decide that you are always divinely protected. Choose peaceful energy so you don't have to defend yourself.
>
> **CHAKRA(S):** Crown, third eye
>
> **ELEMENT(S):** Fire
>
> **PAIRS WELL WITH:** Amethyst and smoky quartz are beneficial for discernment, protection, and grounding. To bring truth to the forefront, wear amazonite in a bracelet or carry a tumbled stone. Inhale the aroma of frankincense essential oil or incense to stabilize your spiritual practice in your daily life. A crown chakra essential oil blend can be used to increase your connection with

divine consciousness and your intuition. Purple-dyed agate also pairs with Archangel Azrael, the angel of comfort and death. Azrael helps people transition from their earthly bodies during death.

NOTES: Because purple-dyed agate is man-made, this stone is not water safe. The dye will leak out if this stone comes in contact with water and could stain the surface it is on.

Crystals for Meditation

Meditation is a great way to calm your mind and emotions. Enjoy sparkling treasures from the earth to increase your awareness of the present moment. Clear your mind with **apophyllite**, **clear quartz**, or **selenite** and then use your breath to amplify the glowing light around you and within. **Amethyst** is ideal for activating the third eye and crown chakras. Visualize the purple light of amethyst around you to transform chaotic thoughts and dissipate stress. The golden flecks of **pyrite** found in the deep, rich blue of **lapis lazuli** are perfect for connecting with the sparkles of light around the crown of the head and grounding the experience.

Crystals for Reiki Practitioners

◆

Stilbite is an excellent partner for Reiki practitioners. It increases the acceptance of holistic therapies. **Apophyllite** helps with all types of spiritual healing, as it brings higher levels of clarity and connection with the Divine. **Celestite** is a stone of heavenly communication. Use it to reduce mental chatter and calm turbulent emotions and feelings. **Peridot** increases the benefits of Reiki sessions. It helps transform negative emotions like agitation, impatience, and jealousy.

Pyrite

chapter three

Pyrite increases luminescence around you by activating the golden flecks in your energy field. Use it to amplify the sparkle in your halo—your crown chakra. Pyrite is the perfect stone for grounding your spiritual life because it offers a strong foundation, as it naturally grows in block formations. This is a stone of financial abundance; pyrite is an excellent tool for amplifying your success, reaching your goals, and witnessing the realization of your intentions.

> **DIVINATORY MEANING:** It's time to earn unlimited income doing what you love. Contemplate how you manage the order of tasks in your life from start to finish. You have many skills, and you have what you need to be successful—follow your dreams!
>
> **CHAKRA(S):** Root, sacral, solar plexus, crown
>
> **ELEMENT(S):** Fire, air
>
> **PAIRS WELL WITH:** Vetiver essential oil is a powerful aid for relaxation and the sense of being grounded. Other stones like copper, galena (lead), hematite, rutilated quartz, sunstone, and tiger iron have a similar vibe and will add energy to your use of pyrite. Use pyrite to connect with Archangel Uriel to aid you on your spiritual and intellectual journey toward wisdom. *Clematis* Bach Flower Remedy is ideal for maintaining focus

on the present moment. You can combine pyrite with citrine, green aventurine, and/or jade to activate prosperity and gift-giving attributes. Affirm, "I have plenty of money and plenty to share."

NOTES: This silvery or brassy stone, known as "fool's gold," forms in the cubic system. It grows with other minerals like galena, sphalerite, and chalcopyrite. This stone is not water safe. Pyrite will rust or change color if there is extended exposure to water.

Red Jasper

chapter three

Red jasper is an ideal stone for instant manifestation. Its key phrase is "Manifesto presto!" Red jasper is your ally when you are working on manifesting on any level: mentally, emotionally, physically, or spiritually. Use red jasper to motivate yourself, ending procrastination. With red jasper in hand, take unwavering action toward any goal. This is a stone of endurance, so use red jasper to reactivate your zealousness for life. Red jasper will also ground you as you move forward. Intense focus is key; consciously connect with gratitude that your basic needs are met. Use red jasper to promote well-being and inner strength.

> **DIVINATORY MEANING:** Speak up for yourself. Put your plan into action. It's time to follow through. You can and will make this happen. Feel the vital life force that flows through you. You are stable and unwavering in your actions.
>
> **CHAKRA(S):** Root, sacral
>
> **ELEMENT(S):** Fire, earth
>
> **PAIRS WELL WITH:** Instant manifestation is possible when you visualize the outcome and pair red jasper with emerald, garnet, carnelian, Mookaite jasper, ruby, and ruby in zoisite. To help manifest goals that feel like miracles, inhale jasmine and rose essential oils to

call upon Mother Mary, Saint Jude, and Saint Thérèse of Lisieux. Focus on financial success and passionate action. Archangel Ariel helps to increase motivation, vitality, and vigor.

NOTES: Jasper is opaque and comes in many colors, such as yellow, brown, green, and varying shades of red. The red color is due to iron inclusions. This stone is water safe.

Crystals to Clear the Monkey Mind

"Monkey mind" is a Buddhist concept and animal metaphor describing a restless, chattering mind. Releasing difficult-to-control thoughts and finding focus can bring inner peace. Meditation and mindfulness go hand in hand. Instill a practice of being truly present in the moment. With **amethyst, black tourmaline, hematite**, or **lapis lazuli** nearby, focus on your breath—the inhalation and the exhalation. Stay aware of the flow of your breath to relax your mind.

Crystals for Intuition: Clairaudience

◆

Clairaudience is the ability to hear what isn't audible with the physical ears, receiving messages and information from within as well as divine sources. Crystals that help with mindfulness and the throat chakra support clairaudience: The rich turquoise colors of **amazonite** align you with the truth of any matter and ease in expressing the truth, and the pastel blue shade of **angelite** supports communication with the higher realms of consciousness. I also recommend stones that are grounding and potentially magnetized, like **hematite** and **lodestone**, to bring forth clear clairaudient messages. Use these gems to trust the voice within.

Rose Quartz

chapter three

Rose quartz is the ultimate stone for love, friendship, and community. Let its pink vibration add the element of love to your thoughts and to all that you do. Use rose quartz to practice thinking through your heart; this stone aligns your consciousness with divine love, compassion, mercy, tolerance, and kindness. Keep rose quartz nearby when you need to feel comfort and unconditional love. With rose quartz in hand, it is easy to call on the energy of the angels. This stone is also beneficial for skin rejuvenation and regeneration.

> **DIVINATORY MEANING:** Cultivate friendship and romance. Allow the feeling of love within you and around you. Take time to rejuvenate your physical body—you are loved. Let the love keep you healthy and youthful.
>
> **CHAKRA(S):** Heart
>
> **ELEMENT(S):** Water
>
> **PAIRS WELL WITH:** Danburite, green aventurine, jade, kunzite, pink calcite, rhodochrosite, rhodonite, serpentine, and watermelon tourmaline are heart chakra stones that can be used to amplify the positive effects of rose quartz. Jasmine, lavender, rose, and sweet marjoram essential oils are excellent for adding another element of love and increasing the benefits of rose quartz. Call on Flamingo as an animal ally when you are ready

to enjoy the company of good friends. Flamingo is also the perfect ally to call on if you are trying to attract a monogamous life partner. Invite Archangels Chamuel and Jophiel to attract unconditional love in your life.

NOTES: This pink quartz has been used since ancient times. This stone is water safe. However, avoid submerging rose quartz in water for extended periods.

Ruby

chapter three

Ruby, the red variety of the mineral corundum, is a precious stone. It can help you get fired up and increase enthusiasm. If you need motivation, keep ruby nearby to complete tasks that you've been putting off. Ruby can be used to transform stagnant energy and limiting belief systems because it sparks your inner strength and passion for life. Its fiery red energy connects you with what is important and helps you take action to pursue it. Use ruby with visualization to attract happy relationships, as ruby magnetizes your spiritually aligned life partner.

>   **DIVINATORY MEANING:** Take steps to improve your health and endurance by shifting from lethargy to action. Create a mental passion for life. Be more outgoing and willing to connect with others. Embrace your magnificence and live life passionately. Allow love into your life; you are blessed with great friends and family.

CHAKRA(S): Root

ELEMENT(S): Fire

PAIRS WELL WITH: Ruby in zoisite and ruby in fuchsite are excellent amplifiers of ruby's benefits. *Gentian* and *Hornbeam* Bach Flower Remedies help clear blocks and activate self-motivation. Ginger and patchouli essential oils increase motivation and relieve apathy. Inhale ginger to remember that you can create and transform your reality with your mind. Hold positive thoughts to increase these benefits, such as *I am self-motivated and productive. I complete tasks with ease.*

NOTES: Rubies are most prized in their red color, but keep a lookout for ruby in colors like pink, orange, and purple. This stone is not water safe.

Crystals for Health and Healing

◆

Many gemstones can help with overall vitality. Crystals that support better eating habits and digestion are **apatite**, **citrine**, **malachite**, and **peridot**. Most red stones, like **garnet**, **red jasper**, and **ruby**, will help motivate you to move your body. **Azurite** and **chrysocolla** support regeneration and recuperation. The best crystals to have nearby at bedtime are **amethyst** for dreaming, **blue calcite** for peace, **hematite** for protection and grounding, **rose quartz** for comfort and love, and **selenite** for vibrationally surrounding yourself with white light. With some good rest under your belt, use orange and red gemstones like **carnelian**, **red calcite**, and **Mookaite jasper** for vitality.

Crystals for Massage Therapists

Selenite and **orange calcite** are excellent crystal allies for massage therapists and their clients. These stones amplify the benefits of treatment and align with proper care of the muscles, bones, nerves, and tendons. They also strengthen the core physical structure of the body. Orange calcite helps process feelings stored in your body, so use it to release discomfort in the muscles and tendons. **Sardonyx** provides stabilization, strength, endurance, energy, and fortitude. **Leopardskin jasper**, a stone of flexibility, is good for muscles and tendons.

Selenite

chapter three

Selenite, a form of gypsum, glows and shimmers in light, which helps increase your ability to see things more clearly. Selenite is beneficial for mental clarity, brightening your outlook and opening your mind to unlimited possibilities. This stone is named after the moon goddess, Selene, so use the vibration of selenite to be in tune with the moon's cycles. Allow the light of this stone to raise your awareness and support your personal development. You can use selenite to clear and recharge other crystals, including crystal jewelry. It is often found in disc form, which can then be used as a charging plate for anything you want to clear and charge. Keep a stick or log of selenite at your home's front and rear entrances to establish sacred space. Selenite is a stone of alignment and helps you align mentally, emotionally, physically, and spiritually.

> DIVINATORY MEANING: Tune in to the wisdom of the higher realms of consciousness. You have access to all the answers within. Listen and connect with lovingkindness. Shine your light and be a brilliant example of compassionate action.
>
> CHAKRA(S): All
>
> ELEMENT(S): Water
>
> PAIRS WELL WITH: Selenite pairs well with all crystals, as it will amplify and charge any stone. One particularly

beneficial combination is kyanite and selenite, which will help align your chakras and awaken intuitive abilities. To sanctify your space, use sandalwood essential oil, fragrance, incense, or resin.

NOTES: Shiny white, translucent selenite is easy to find. It can be found as peach selenite, also known as red selenite or orange selenite, due to iron oxide impurities present during the formation of the stone. This stone is not water safe.

Smoky Quartz

chapter three

Smoky quartz is an excellent aid to heal old emotional wounds. Smoky quartz is your ally when you've decided to release bad habits and patterns; it's a good companion during the process of getting sober. Smoky quartz is a protective stone. Keep a piece nearby when healing trauma. It's grounding and helps energetically cauterize emotional wounds and traumatic memories. Use smoky quartz to be present in every moment and heighten situational awareness.

> **DIVINATORY MEANING:** Pay attention to the signs and symbols around you, increasing situational awareness. Create circumstances of safety and protection. Ground yourself and feel your connection with all that is. Eliminate doubt and worry—keep your attention on what is essential.
>
> **CHAKRA(S):** Root
>
> **ELEMENT(S):** Earth
>
> **PAIRS WELL WITH:** Inhale sweet marjoram essential oil to quiet your emotions, fears, and paranoias (known and unknown).[2] Sweet marjoram creates a protective vibration around you; use it to feel safe, heal from addictions, and release phobias. Charoite and sodalite pair

---

2. Sweet marjoram naturally lowers your blood pressure, so use it sparingly or not at all if you have low blood pressure.

well with smoky quartz to remove anger and negative forces within and around you. Ask Archangels Michael and Jehudiel to support you with your challenges.

NOTES: This translucent brown or black quartz is found naturally in the earth. Smoky quartz can also be irradiated (treated with cobalt 60 and electrons) and then heated to enhance or create the smoky brown color; the resulting look is an opaque black or brown. This stone is water safe.

Crystals and Essential Oils for Health and Well-Being

Chamomile and **angelite** increase the power of intention to release the past and feel the good in your life. Use them together for comfort and peace. Chamomile, a calming essential oil, supports peaceful sleep and dreaming. Angelite's heavenly blue color increases serenity and heals frayed nerves. Angelite and chamomile will help you release negative emotions and bring calm. *Avoid chamomile if allergic to asters, daisies, chrysanthemums, or ragweed. Do not use if pregnant or nursing.*

Crystals for Intuition: Clairolfaction

◆

Clairolfaction is the ability to smell a scent or aroma that doesn't have a physical source or isn't detectable by others. Odors picked up this way often signal the presence of spirit. For example, smelling cigarette or cigar smoke might signal a visitation from a loved one on the other side; rose or incense-like aromas could be a saint, spiritual guide, or angel. **Blue lace agate**, **blue aragonite**, and **blue chalcedony** support the olfactory nerve on a metaphysical level. **Green moss agate** and **tree agate** bring clarity surrounding psychic messages.

Sodalite

Sodalite is a calming and grounding gem that is good for inspiration, intuition, spiritual alignment, and writing. It is a great stone for reducing the constant chatter in your mind. Sodalite is a writer's ally, as it can help you maintain focus on completing a project. This is also an excellent stone to use to improve your psychic skills. Gaze at sodalite to calm your thoughts and reduce anger and vindictive vibes. Sodalite has a cooling vibration, so it can assist in balancing your emotions. Work with sodalite when you feel an emotional outburst coming on. Sodalite has a protective quality, and it is ideal when calling on archangels to support you daily.

DIVINATORY MEANING: Make meditation a regular part of your day. Visualize your outcomes and find inner peace through the knowing you have. Tranquility is yours. Maintain a sense of calm for better results in all aspects of your life.

CHAKRA(S): Crown, third eye, root

ELEMENT(S): Earth

PAIRS WELL WITH: Call on Archangel Michael and Mother Mary to help strengthen your faith in life. Combine sodalite with lapis lazuli to increase your intuition and open a channel to higher wisdom. Sodalite is a good stone for connecting with many archangels, especially

Gabriel and Sandalphon. Pair sodalite with indicolite (blue tourmaline), iolite, and sapphire to organize your thoughts and achieve a single-minded focus. Employ the Bach Flower Remedies *Impatiens* for patience and *White Chestnut* for inner peace.

NOTES: Sodalite is dark blue with white calcite inclusions and black veins caused by hydrothermal fluids creating crystallization. This stone is water safe, but do not submerge it in water for an extended period.

Sugilite

chapter three

Sugilite can help you improve your intuitive abilities, especially clairolfaction and clairaudience; therefore, it is a good ally for spiritual counselors and tarot readers. Sugilite is an excellent tool for releasing negative experiences because it helps you let go of the past and move forward in a positive way. Stare at this purple rock when you want to transform your personal life. The transmutational power of purple transforms unwanted belief systems, gently guiding you toward more beneficial belief systems. On a physical level, sugilite helps support endurance and healthy lungs. It can be beneficial for those overcoming iron deficiency. Sugilite is also a good companion stone when learning to embrace happiness and inner peace; keep it nearby to cultivate loving-kindness with healthy detachment.

> **DIVINATORY MEANING:** Step away from situations that cause friction or challenges. Let go of judgments of yourself and others. Visualize a calm and peaceful life. You have inner peace and true happiness, and you find them within you. Relax and find ways to comfort yourself.
>
> **CHAKRA(S):** Crown, third eye
>
> **ELEMENT(S):** Air
>
> **PAIRS WELL WITH:** The animal ally Pig pairs with sugilite for forward movement after releasing negative experi-

ences. Pigs cannot move their necks to look back, so they can't see behind them without turning around; in this way, Pig symbolically reminds you to move forward and not look back. Vetiver essential oil is especially beneficial to clear your energy field and ground you.

NOTES: Sugilite, a semiprecious stone, is a striking purple color. This stone is water safe. Avoid soaking for extended periods to keep from ruining the finish.

Crystals for Intuition: Clairvoyance

◆

Clairvoyance is the ability to see what can't be seen by the physical eyes, often through inner sight, visions, or interpretation of symbols in daily life. Clear, white, and translucent stones help with clarity. **Apophyllite, clear quartz**, and **optical calcite** are superb because of the stones' transparency. Purple stones like **amethyst, charoite**, or **sugilite** are good allies for interpreting the meanings of dreams and visions. Dark blue stones are helpful to maintain a quiet mind and release incessant chatter that can interrupt insight. Work with **blue tiger's eye** (also known as hawk's eye), **lapis lazuli**, and **sodalite** to clear your mind.

Crystals for Inner Harmony and Peace

◆

Having inner harmony and peace is a choice you can make. It's up to you to find the place within you that is stable, peaceful, and filled with love and kindness. Gemstones that promote calm vibrations are **blue calcite**, **blue lace agate**, and **morganite**. Create inner peace through self-care using **chrysoprase**. With **danburite** and **kunzite**, improve self-love and your ability to set boundaries with kindness and grace.

Tiger's Eye

chapter three

Tiger's eye is known for deflecting the evil eye. The chatoyant nature of this stone makes it a perfect tool to deflect jealousy and any energy that is not for your highest good. Tiger's eye is also helpful for keeping your own feelings of jealousy at bay. Use this protective stone to keep your energy field bright and light. Tiger's eye improves your ability to see on all levels: mentally, emotionally, spiritually, and physically. Pair this gemstone with the intention to improve your vital life force and your feelings of self-empowerment. Tiger's eye is the perfect stone to boost your self-esteem and confidence, and gold tiger's eye is especially beneficial for improving your outlook on life.

DIVINATORY MEANING: See all that is good in your life. Contemplate your blessings and watch them multiply. Be happy for your good fortune *and* the good fortune that others experience. Radiate goodness and well-being, and have pure intentions in all that you do.

CHAKRA(S): Solar plexus, sacral, root

ELEMENT(S): Fire

PAIRS WELL WITH: Grapefruit, lemon, orange, and petitgrain essential oils help awaken a sunny outlook on life. The best method is to inhale one or all of these citrus essential oils. If these essential oils are diluted and used topically, keep in mind that they are phototoxic; therefore, avoid exposure to direct sunlight while they are on your skin. Affirm good thoughts like "I have the courage and confidence to shine my light and be all that I can be."

NOTES: This brown and gold banded stone is perfect for protection. It can also be found in honey, blue, and red hues. This stone is water safe. Avoid soaking it for extended periods to keep from ruining the finish.

Unakite

chapter three

Unakite combines pink feldspar and green epidote, making it a perfect stone for opening your heart to love and kindness. Work with unakite to improve your relationships with everyone you interact with. It is a stone of compassion and tolerance. Use unakite to gently balance your emotions and detach from drama. Let the peachy-pink colors of unakite inspire a deeper connection with compassion and love. This stone's olive-green colors help integrate life experiences, aiding in the integration and digestion of life. Gaze at unakite to encourage your consciousness to heal digestive challenges, which are often directly related to emotional distress.

> **DIVINATORY MEANING:** It's time to take care of yourself. Find your favorite nurturing activities and comfort your emotional body. Embrace your emotions. You are a caring person—care for yourself as much as you care for others.
>
> **CHAKRA(S):** Heart, solar plexus, sacral
>
> **ELEMENT(S):** Earth, water
>
> **PAIRS WELL WITH:** Invoke the Angel of Balanced Emotions to reduce emotional outbursts and let go. Archangels Chamuel and Jophiel can be invoked to free you of past emotional challenges and open yourself up to loving relationships. *Rock Water* Bach Flower Remedy

helps bring balance. Animal allies like Cat, Crab, Otter, and Penguin can also bring balance to your feelings and emotions. Other gems that work well with unakite are peridot, prehnite, prasiolite, and rose quartz.

NOTES: This stone is water safe for short periods. Avoid prolonged submersion.

Crystals to Connect with Nature

Nature therapy brings balance to the tech world we live in. Spend some time in nature and allow the peaceful environment and the smells of the earth, sea, and sky to relieve stress. It's very simple: Sit or stand outside in the shade or the sun. Breathe and be in the present moment. **Selenite, desert rose**, and **petrified wood** will help you align with the origins and history of the earth. To connect with plants, trees, and shrubs, use **green moss agate** and **tree agate**. Stones that connect with bodies of water like streams, rivers, and oceans include **aquamarine, enhydro quartz**, and **larimar**. You can connect with gnomes, elves, salamanders, fairies, and undines using **andalusite (chiastolite), aquamarine, brown agate, green tourmaline, llanite (rhyolite)**, and **opal**.

Conclusion

I hope you find support and alliance with the world of crystals and gemstones. Find comfort in knowing that you have all the help you need to overcome any challenge you might experience.

Remember, every thought, word, feeling, and action create your reality. Pair your good thoughts with specific stones to amplify what you are creating. Pairing crystals with affirmations helps you achieve your goals and desires. Allow yourself to use all the spiritual tools available to you, from aromatherapy to animal allies to archangels and saints. With mindfulness and crystal-clear intentions, you have the tools to be all that you can be.

My wish for you is that you will be happy, feel love, be compassionate and kind, and have an abundance of prosperity and blessings in your life.

Recommended Reading

Here are some books I recommend for learning more about spirituality. I've included books by other authors that I've used and enjoyed as well as books I've written.

Crystals

Chakra Awakening: Transform Your Reality Using Crystals, Color, Aromatherapy & the Power of Positive Thought by Margaret Ann Lembo

Crystal Enlightenment: The Transforming Properties of Crystals and Healing Stones by Katrina Raphaell

Crystal Healing: The Therapeutic Application of Crystals and Stones by Katrina Raphaell

The Crystalline Transmission: A Synthesis of Light by Katrina Raphaell

Crystals Beyond Beginners: Awaken Your Consciousness with Precious Gifts from the Earth by Margaret Ann Lembo

The Essential Guide to Crystals, Minerals, and Stones by Margaret Ann Lembo

Love Is in the Earth: A Kaleidoscope of Crystals by Melody

The Women's Book of Healing: Auras, Chakras, Laying On of Hands, Crystals, Gemstones, and Colors by Diane Stein

Essential Oils

The Complete Book of Essential Oils and Aromatherapy, Revised and Expanded: Over 800 Natural, Nontoxic, and Fragrant Recipes to Create Health, Beauty, and Safe Home and Work Environments by Valerie Ann Worwood

Essential Aromatherapy: A Pocket Guide to Essential Oils & Aromatherapy by Susan Worwood and Valerie Ann Worwood

The Essential Guide to Aromatherapy and Vibrational Healing by Margaret Ann Lembo

Essential Oil Safety by Robert Tisserand and Rodney Young

Flower Essences

Bach Flower Therapy: Theory and Practice by Mechthild Scheffer

The Bach Flower Remedies by Edward Bach and F. J. Wheeler

Chakras

Chakra Awakening: Transform Your Reality Using Crystals, Color, Aromatherapy & the Power of Positive Thought by Margaret Ann Lembo

Color and Crystals: A Journey Through the Chakras by Joy Gardner

Vibrational Healing Through the Chakras: With Light, Color, Sound, Crystals, and Aromatherapy by Joy Gardner

Wheels of Light: Chakras, Auras, and the Healing Energy of the Body by Rosalyn L. Bruyere

Angels and Saints

The Angels & Gemstone Guardians Cards by Margaret Ann Lembo

The Archangels & Gemstone Guardians Cards by Margaret Ann Lembo

A Dictionary of Angels: Including the Fallen Angels by Gustav Davidson

The Essential Guide to Archangels and Saints by Margaret Ann Lembo

The Essential Guide to Everyday Angels by Margaret Ann Lembo

Messengers of Love, Light, and Grace: Getting to Know Your Personal Angels by Terry Lynn Taylor

Animal Allies

The 13 Original Clan Mothers: Your Sacred Path to Discovering the Gifts, Talents & Abilities of the Feminine Through the Ancient Teachings of the Sisterhood by Jamie Sams

Animal Speak: The Spiritual & Magical Powers of Creatures Great & Small by Ted Andrews

Animal Totems and the Gemstone Kingdom: Spiritual Connections of Crystal Vibrations and Animal Medicine by Margaret Ann Lembo

Animal-Wise: The Spirit Language and Signs of Nature by Ted Andrews

Dancing with the Wheel: The Medicine Wheel Workbook by Sun Bear, Wabun Wind, and Crysalis Mulligan

Medicine Cards: The Discovery of Power Through the Ways of Animals by Jamie Sams and David Carson